LIBRARY OF CONGRESS
CATALOG CARD NUMBER 90-093266

ISBN NUMBER 1-878087-09-6

PRINTED IN U.S.A.

DAVID J. GINGERY PUBLISHING LLC
P.O. BOX 318
ROGERSVILLE, MO 65742

Web: http://www.gingerybooks.com

Email: gingery@gingerybooks.com

CONTENTS

IN MEMORY OF FLOYD CAMPBELL
OF CAMPBELL TOOLS CO.

FOREWORD

I know that I am not the first to suggest that FOREWORD is a misnomer. But
each time I have written a book or article I discover during the editing
process a number of things I wish I had said in the text. Since the pages
are already made up and I am always past such arbitrary deadlines as I tend
to impose on myself it becomes neccessary to figure out some way to tuck in
additional comments without doing the whole job over again. AFTERWORD
would seem out of place at the beginning of a book so I will again resort
to the traditional author's ploy and slip my hindsights in here.

This project was designed to use only the commonest of materials but many
of the simplest items can be difficult to find in some areas. To list the
many excellent mail order supply sources would have made the text
cumbersome so I abandoned that idea. Instead I suggest that you subscribe
to THE HOME SHOP MACHINIST magazine, which regularely carries ads from all
of the best sources. Write to them at PO Box 1810, Traverse City, MI 49685
for subscription rates. If you are uncertain about subscribing ask for the
rate on a single back issue. Once you see this excellent magazine you will
want to subscribe.

WARNING

THERE ARE SERIOUS HAZARDS IN THE PROCESSES AND PROCEDURES IN THIS BOOK. NO
ATTEMPT HAS BEEN MADE TO POINT OUT ALL OF THE DANGERS OR EVEN A MAJORITY OF
THEM. THE AUTHOR IS NOT AN ENGINEER OR SCIENTIST AND NO CLAIM IS MADE TO
THE PROPRIETY OF THE METHODS SUGGESTED IN THESE PAGES. THE READER IS FULLY
RESPONSIBLE FOR DEVISING SAFE PROCEDURES FOR EVERY OPERATION.

PREFACE

A BRIEF HISTORY OF THE STIRLING CYCLE

Many people were working on heat engine mechanisms around the turn of the 19th century. In Great Britain one Sir George Cayley is said to have invented the hot-air engine in 1807 while exploring a variety of propulsion units for aircraft. In American literature credit for the invention is given to Reverend Robert Stirling, a Scottish minister and well known classical scholar of his time. He was 26 years old in 1816 and newly ordained to his first parish when he introduced the world to his engine. Among his many achievements he also became known as the father of the Church of Scotland.

It may be worth pausing to note that being a scholar in 1816 was vastly different than being a student today. Those basic skills of reading, writing and arithmetic that we take for granted in our time were not the common lot in 1816. And certainly the scientific equipment that is everywhere available today was not yet heard of in those times. But while an education was a special privilege of the "nobility" it was not a free gift as it is today. A rigid and stern discipline demanded total dedication and hard work. It must have seemed like anything but a privilege to those who submitted to it.

Robert Stirling was just one in a family line of notable inventors. His grandfather, Michael Stirling, invented the first rotary threshing machine in 1756. His brother, James, was a well recognized civil engineer and four of his sons became engineers of some fame.

No doubt there were many whose efforts and discoveries were not recorded. And certainly not everything was learned or revealed for research continues to the present time. In the 19th century hot-air engines were low in power and speed. A very large bore and stroke produced only a fraction of one horse power at perhaps 200 revolutions per minute. Today high-power, high-speed engines are being built to power generators, manufacturing machinery and, most recently, submarines for specialized work on off-shore oil rigs.

The hot-air engine principle was a natural step in the development of engineering science and it was widely discussed at the time. Much was yet to be discovered and a language was being developed to express the ideas involved. It is reported that Michael Faraday once became confused while delivering a lecture on hot-air engines and was obliged to admit that he could not explain why they ran at all. If you are not thoroughly familiar with the phenomenon you will surely sympathize with his quandary. However we now have the advantage of a well developed language and refined graphic arts to describe and illustrate such ideas. And development of engineering science is by no means completed so these principles are still worthy of discussion and study.

Steam power engineering was ascending in that period and it was the prime mover in every area of industry and transportation. However steam engines and boilers are very dangerous, and costly to produce as well. The world is always ready for a simpler, cheaper and safer source of power for industry and agriculture. Hot-air engines promised much by their simplicity, cheapness and especially the lack of a high pressure boiler. Remember that a steam engine requires a large volume of steam at high pressure. And other problems such as replenishing boiler water, condensation in steam lines and cylinders, scale accumulation, boiler corrosion and much more demanded trained engineers for their operation and maintenance. But a hot-air engine could be operated by anyone who could light a fire. And once started it could be left to run for long periods without attention. Many people experimented with hot-air engines trying to discover improvements in power, efficiency and economy. The main focus of attention was on regenerators and raising the pressure of the air. A great many were manufactured and many of these century old engines can still be found in operating condition everywhere in the world today.

Another who contributed much to the advancement of the hot-air engine principle was John Ericsson, who was 13 years old when Stirling introduced his engine to the world. He was best known in his time as the engineer who designed the civil war battleship, MONITOR, built for the U.S. Navy. And who has not heard of the battle of THE MERRIMAC AND THE MONITOR?

Ericsson was born in Sweden in 1803, moved to England when he was 23 and came to the U.S. when he was 35 to remain for the rest of his life. As well as being a world-famous engineer he was known for amazing physical strength and a fierce temper. As a young man in the Swedish Navy he was said to have lifted a 600 pound canon. Whatever his merits and faults, he was a prolific inventor.

Among his inventions were a practical screw propellor, a steam powered fire engine and some portable tools using compressed air. The forced draft boiler and surface condenser greatly improved performance of steam powered ships. He developed an early depth sounding device which was vital for navigation. He moved the vital machinery of naval ships below the water line and developed the revolving gun turret as well as many other improvements in naval weapons.

But all of Ericsson's achievements were not in war machinery. The 2200 ton ship, ERICSSON, was 250 feet long, driven by side paddle wheels and powered by a four cylinder hot-air engine. The pistons were 14 feet in diameter with a stroke of six feet. Being very slow in operation, it was possible for people to stand on the pistons and ride up and down. For one as prone to seasickness as I it would have been a disaster to be on the ship at all, not to mention riding one of those pistons up and down! But imagine the great accomplishment of casting and machining such large cylinders and pistons at a time in history when most of us suppose the world lived in dismal ignorance! The first engines in the ERICSSON proved too slow to compete with steam engines so new engines were built and installed. The ship sank on its second maiden voyage. Though Ericsson said that the new engines were a success, steam engines were installed when it was raised and returned to service.

In 1872 Ericsson developed a solar version of the Stirling engine and by 1875 he had built seven of them. A solar plant using a Stirling engine with a parabolic reflector was proposed for Phoenix Arizona in 1908. It seems highly likely that this type of engine could be the means to convert both solar and nuclear energy to a useful form in the future. Certainly a goal worth striving for in an era of diminishing fossil fuel rescource!

By 1880 the Ericsson Pumping engine was perfected and patented. They were manufactured in great quantity and marketed around the world until the early 1900's. Many are still found in working condition. The Rider-Ericsson Engine Co. published a list of testimonials in 1906 that included J.P. Morgan of New York, Several of the Vanderbilts, King Edward VII, Andrew Carnegie, The Sultan of Turkey and Valentine Blatz of Milwaukee.

From about 1860 until the first world war hot-air engines in many forms were built and marketed in great quantities for pumping water, ventillating, operating sewing machines, winches, printing presses and as toy and demonstration engines. Of course it was the advent of cheap electricity and the electric motor that displaced the steam-engine, the gas-engine and the hot-air-engine at the point of individual use. But it is worthy of consideration that the majority of the world population today does not yet have cheap electrical power at their disposal, so perhaps these principles are not as obsolete as was supposed.

The purpose of this manual is to present these principles once again, both as an instructive and entertaining project and for research and development as a practical power unit.

THE RIDER-ERICSSON PUMPING ENGINE

3

Whether you are a newcomer to the metal-working crafts or a battle scarred veteran you will appreciate the broad scope of any engine building project. For the student or other beginner it offers a full range of learning exercises and plenty of practical experience. And for the advanced craftsman it provides opportunity to perfect and fine-tune already acquired skills. For all who undertake and complete such a project the reward will be a mechanical marvel to amaze yourself and all others who see it.

Although the Stirling Cycle principle has been thoroughly researched and documented since its inception in 1816 it is not well known today except by relatively few. Having been generally dismissed as obsolete since early in this century, it is again appearing as the power plant in some interesting applications. In fact some have suggested that it could well be the engine of the future. So we are not dealing with obsolete and archaic technology, but rather with a re-emerging technology based upon solid principles of physics and mechanics. It will prove a fascinating study to merely learn how it operates in the first place. And those who actually build it will apply processes of pattern-making, molding and pouring castings, layout and bench-work, drilling, boring, reaming, lapping, threading, tapping and myriads of metal-lathe and shop operations that will build skill and confidence while yielding the parts for the engine. Whether a beginning or advanced metal-worker, you will be a better craftsman when this project is done.

The specific design presented in this manual was concieved while building a single cylinder engine originally presented by Mr. T. E. Haynes of Great Britain in a small book published by John Murray. Originally published in Great Britain in 1966, it was later reprinted in the U.S. by Caldwell Industries in 1978. I regret that the book does not seem to be available in the U.S. at this writing for it was an excellent project.

This design is not offered as a practical ideal but rather as a model and demonstration engine. The greater value of the project lies first in the many learning and skill building exercises and second in a working engine that demonstrates physical and mechanical principles with which to begin to design a far better engine. Of course the design can be merely increased in size for greater power but that would only affirm what has already been proven. Probably the more productive line of experimentation would be in the area of gasses other than air, higher internal pressures, faster acting linkages and more efficient heat transfer. Amazing strides have been made since 1816 and there is much left to discover.

THE WORKING PRINCIPLE

It is a well established principle of physics that gasses expand in volume when heated and that they contract when cooled. Confined to a limited area, the heated expanding gas will increase in pressure and the pressure will drop when it is cooled. Air is a readily available mixture of gasses for a rudimentary engine but other gasses are known to work much more efficiently.

In the Stirling Cycle process these changing pressures are applied to the power piston to cause it to reciprocate in its cylinder and turn the flywheel through a connecting rod and crankshaft.

Very simply, the change in pressure is accomplished by sweeping the gas back and forth in a closed cylinder that is heated at one end and cooled at the other. The closed cylinder may be vertical or horizontal or at any angle. And it may be separate from the power cylinder or an extension of it. A tube or passage admits the changing pressures to the power piston when the transfer cylinder is separate.

So for discussion we refer to the transfer piston and transfer cylinder where the pressures are changed, and to the power piston and power cylinder where the changing pressures are put to work. The transfer piston is connected to the power piston through linkage in order to maintain a phase relationship so that pressure is applied and relieved at the proper instant. Theoretically the transfer piston leads the power piston by 90 degrees. But the practical optimum turns out to be 80 or less degrees in actual practice. The object of course is to reach the highest possible pressure as the power piston travels towards the crankshaft and the lowest possible pressure as it travels away from the crankshaft. An internal view of one pair of cylinders will help to clarify.

Notice in figure 1 that the power piston is at top dead center and the transfer piston is midway in its travel. Half of the air in the transfer cylinder has been displaced towards the hot end and it has begun to expand and increase in pressure. In figure 2 the transfer piston has reached the end of its travel and all but a tiny amount of the air has been displaced to the hot end. Pressure is now at its maximum as the power piston is forced towards bottom dead center. In figure 3 the power piston is at bottom dead center and the transfer piston is already half way towards the hot end so that the air is displaced towards the cool end to drop the pressure. In figure 4 all but a tiny part of the air has been displaced to the cool end so that pressure is at its lowest as the flywheel carries the power piston towards top dead center to begin the cycle over again. Of course the opposite event occurs in the other pair of cylinders at each moment.

It is truly amazing to see this rudimentary engine run at speeds of hundreds of revolutions per minute and to realize that the expansion and contraction of the heated and cooled air occurs so rapidly. But modern Stirling Cycle engines now run at thousands of revolutions per minute and deliver great power with astounding efficiency. In addition they are very clean operating and adaptable to fuels and heat sources not practical for internal combusion engines. So these principles bear close scrutiny in our age. See how idealy these principles apply to solar and nuclear power, and as well as to conventional fuels so long as they remain available.

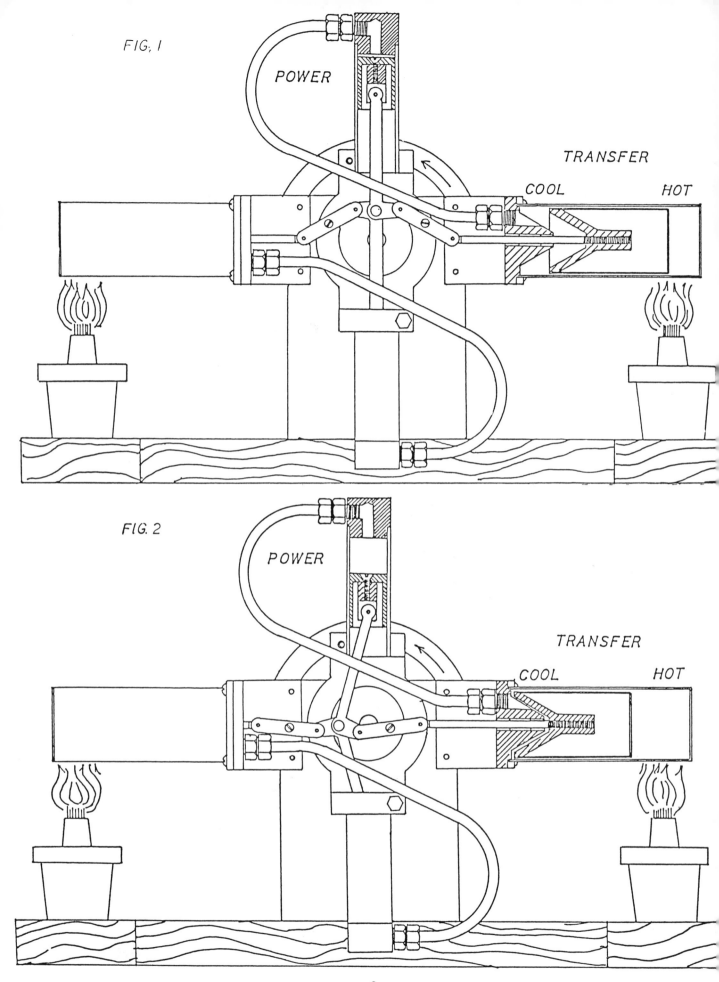

FIG; I

POWER

TRANSFER

COOL   HOT

FIG. 2

POWER

TRANSFER

COOL   HOT

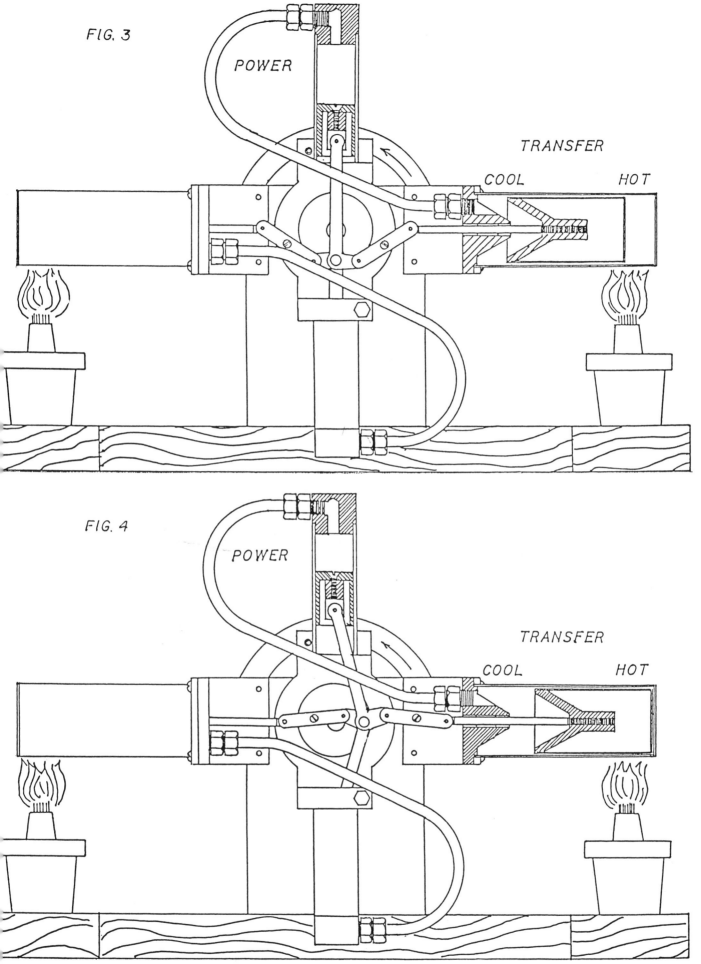

FIG. 3

POWER

TRANSFER

COOL   HOT

FIG. 4

POWER

TRANSFER

COOL   HOT

HOW THE ENGINE IS BUILT

This is essentially a metal lathe project and every part could actually be
made from scrap materials providing that large enough pieces of aluminum
were available. But that would be extremely wasteful of material and time
and it will be a more satisfying and rewarding project if castings are used
for most of the parts. At the time of this writing some are planning to
offer casting kits and that is certainly a practical way to go. But for
the more ambitious and dedicated craftsman we include the details of
patterns and molds to produce your own castings.

Possibly the most intimidating aspect of the project would be the
production of the castings. There is rather wide-spread belief that the
foundry craft is highly technical, dreadfully dangerous, very costly and
simply not practical on a small scale. Actually the obstacles are badly
overstated and I hope to pursuade you that adding these simple skills and
processes to your repertoire will greatly expand your metal-working shop
experience. A rudimentary foundry operation can turn out many sets of
castings at extremely low cost so that this and many other projects become
affordable. If you do not already have a foundry setup you can easily put
one together with the aid of a number of good books on the topic. You can
also purchase small units ideal for the home shop from Pyramid Products Co.
3736 South 7th Ave., Phoenix, AZ 85041.

It is true that there are specific dangers in foundry work just as there
are in all other shop occupations. Certainly working with tempratures high
enough to melt metals will involve unusual risks and require precautions.
And I hasten to add for the sake of the young and inexperienced student
that adult guidance and supervision are essential in all of the operations
in this book. The mere fact that you can read and understand the
directions is not sufficient because there is much about shop safety that
is not discussed. We will discuss shop safety in some detail a little
later.

A sturdy work bench with a hefty vise will be used throughout the project.
The usual assortment of hand tools including hacksaw, files, scriber,
square, rule, micrometer or vernier calipers, drills, reamers etc. will be
required. A lathe will be required for most of the operations. The
flywheel and the stand will require a swing in excess of 3 1/2 inches but
remaining parts can be done on a smaller machine. Although I have not done
so I think that all of the parts could be machined on a Sherline, Unimat or
Taig lathe with the aid of raising blocks. All of the development work was
done on an Atlas 6" swing lathe. An angle plate will be essential in
machining the transfer cylinder mounts so a sturdy spindle and faceplate
mount are vital. A tailstock chuck will be needed for drilling, tapping
and reaming operations. And a tailstock die holder will be needed for
threading the crank pin and the special cap screws. A bench grinder and a
drill press with a drilling vise should complete the equipment list. For
the pattern making operations a table saw is very useful but not entirely
neccessary. The amount of sawing is not great and it could be done with a
hand saw. A belt or disc sander would speed some of the work but again the
volume of work is not so great that it can't be done by hand methods. It
is worth remembering that some means can usually be devised to do the job
even when the preferred equipment is not available.

SAFETY IN THE SHOP

No attempt will be made to point out all of the dangers that may be encountered in this project. You must be very attentive to details and very alert to danger at all times. The correct approach to the topic of safety in any circumstance is to pause long enough to consider potential dangers. You simply contemplate a tool, machine or other device or thing and ask yourself "How can this thing hurt me?" When danger is recognized it is easy to take precautions. The most common injuries in all machine operations are foreign objects in the eye and badly cut or dismembered fingers or hands. If you realized the deadly force with which a carbide tip leaves a saw blade you would never operate a power saw without a blade guard. If you fully realized that a small bit of wood, metal or abrasive can be imbedded in your eye and possibly destroy your vision you would not operate a machine without eye protection. If you realized with what sudden and great force the machine can grab a piece of work and pull your hand into the blade you would always use a push stick and never put your fingers in the area of danger. Long hair or jewelry caught in a machine can cause dreadful injury or death, as can loose fitting clothing. And there are dozens of other hazards that will be apparent to the thoughtful craftsman. Study every item in your shop and fully understand its use. Read the instructions attentively and heed every precaution. Post clear warnings and reminders both for yourself and visitors. Keep the floor swept clear of debris that might cause a stumble. And make sure that every piece of equipment is in top condition. Think each operation through to its end before you begin. And take every precaution to ensure that you do not expose yourself or anyone else to danger.

If you are going to purchase a castings kit you can now skip on to the next chapter. But if you really want to have fun and develop your shop skill begin now to make the patterns and prepare to cast your own.

THE HAYNES ENGINE

CHAPTER I

PRODUCING THE CASTINGS

PATTERN-MAKING BASICS

Our objective in this chapter is to produce the patterns that represent the casting shapes we want. It is assumed that the reader has some knowledge and experience in the foundry crafts and that equipment is on hand to make a mold and pour a casting. If that is not the case some additional reading and preparation will be neccessary before castings can be produced. If you are undecided about whether or not to establish a home foundry perhaps this chapter will help resolve your doubts.

There are many casting processes but in this project we will discuss only sand molding. This involves imbedding a pattern in sand in a two part mold and then removing the pattern to leave a cavity into which molten metal is poured to produce a casting. Because the mold must be opened and closed to remove the pattern, and it must retain the shape of the pattern after it is removed, the sand we use is of a special nature. Obviously dry sand such as found on the beach would not serve the purpose. The grains in molding sand are coated with an adhesive agent so that they will stick together and retain a definite shape. The adhesive agent may be clay and water as in the case of GREEN-SAND, or it may be a petroleum product as in the case of one proprietary brand called PETRO-BOND. Each type has advantages and disadvantages but either will produce satisfactory molds for this project.

In order that the pattern can be easily removed from the mold without damaging it the vertical surfaces are lightly sloped. This is called DRAFT. A draft of one degree is the minimum for a skilled molder. A beginner might require a draft of three to five degrees to ensure a clean mold cavity. And some types of patterns will require greater draft than others even though the shapes are quite simple.

Because molding sand is not very strong at best we avoid creating weak areas in the mold such as very thin and intricate sections. Outside corners are given a RADIUS and inside corners are given a FILLET. That is to say they are rounded off to eliminate sharp angles and edges.

Molten metal shrinks upon solidification and cooling. And castings usually must be machined to their final size. So allowances are made in the pattern for shrinkage and machining. In small, light castings the amount of shrinkage is slight and can usually be ignored or included in the machining allowance. The machining allowance must be adequate to allow for unavoidable eccentricity in mounting and for surface imperfections in the casting. An excess machining allowance will often ensure success but it will greatly lengthen the machining process. The actual allowance must be determined by the quality of available equipment and the skill of the machinist. The allowances suggested in this project assume that the machinist is not highly skilled and equipment may be old and worn. A skilled operator with good equipment can reduce those allowances for greater speed and economy.

Aluminum shrinks approximately 3/16" per foot in all directions so if you want an aluminum casting 12 inches long you would prepare a pattern that is 12 3/16 inches long. A pattern 4 1/16" long would produce a casting 4" long. With the exception of the base casting none of the castings in this project exceed the 4" dimension so shrinkage is not a serious factor.

Close grained hardwood is the ideal pattern material and white pine is readily available and easily worked with ordinary tools and skill. Ordinary white carpenters glue is adequate for joining parts of patterns. I use polyester auto body putty for filling imperfections and for wiping a fillet at the inside corners. After completion and mounting patterns must be painted or varnished to prevent absorption of moisture during use.

Pattern making is a simple process requiring only ordinary skills. You will have little difficulty following the specific directions for each pattern in the following pages.

SOME TRICKS AND TOOLS

It is generally easy to draw an outline and to cut a piece of wood to the desired shape and size and all manner of ordinary tools will serve to do that portion of the job. But since draft is the all important element in pattern making the job becomes a bit more challenging. Of course the blade can be tilted on a table-saw, band-saw or jig-saw. But the resulting cut will be rough and some finishing will be required. A belt or disc sander can be very helpful but is not available in every shop. And some patterns are so small and delicate that even a moments touch on a sanding machine can destroy them. So some means of accurate hand sanding must be used in even the best equipped shops. And some means must be used to determine whether the draft is correct and adequate after finishing. A set of blocks cut to the desired angles will serve to accurately sand drafted surfaces. And a small try-square will enable you to test the angle of draft.

From scraps of common 2 X 4 lumber cut blocks with one side angled as in figure 5. One each with angles of 1 1/2 and 3 degrees will be useful for the patterns in this project. Identify the blocks by printing the angle on the face of each block. The blocks are nominally 1 1/2" square and 4" long. One edge is cut at 90 degrees and the opposite edge is cut at the desired angle. Note that the effect will be an ACUTE angle (less than 90 degrees) on one corner and an OBTUSE angle (greater than 90 degrees) on the other corner. The other two corners will be 90 degrees.

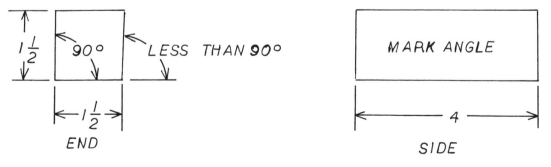

FIGURE 5- ANGLED SANDING BLOCK

In use a sheet of sand paper is laid on the work table and the angled block is used as a guide or fence to hold the workpiece at the desired angle as it is drawn back and forth over the sandpaper as shown in figure 6. Coarse 60 grit paper will serve to rapidly remove stock and 120 grit or finer will serve to finish the surface. The circumstance will determine whether to use the obtuse or acute angle.

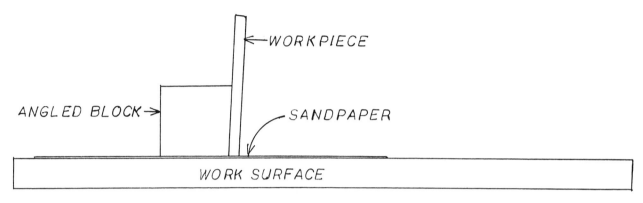

FIGURE 6- USING THE ANGLE BLOCK

Figure 7 illustrates the use of a trysquare to check the draft angle on all vertical surfaces of the pattern.

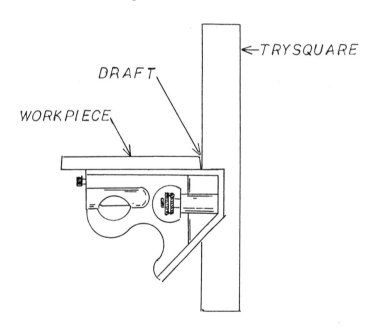

FIGURE 7- CHECKING DRAFT

Simply cutting to shape and size and finishing with the angled sanding blocks will serve for all rectangular shapes. Round shapes can be produced on the lathe and compound shapes can be assembled with glue. In some instances small brads can be used with glued joints to assemble patterns.

Fine sandpaper wrapped around a block of wood works well for rounding over outside corners. The fillets can be wiped into inside corners with the

12

finger and sandpaper can be wrapped around a rod or dowel to finish the surface of the fillets. Polyester auto body putty is an ideal material for such work since it sets up firmly in a short time and it is easily worked for a longer time after initial set. When fully cured it is very durable.

In some instances special tools must be improvised to finish surfaces not easily reached. Small contoured or flat scrapers can easily be made from light sheet metal. And sometimes it works well to simply sharpen the edge of a nail head and fit a dowel for a handle to make a simple scraper.

The important thing to keep in mind is that the patterns must be well drafted and very smooth so that they will withdraw easily from the mold without breaking the edge of the cavity.

In this project some of the patterns will be molded individually and others will be mounted on a board called a MATCH-PLATE. One advantage of using a matchplate is that several patterns can be molded in a single flask, thus saving much time and labor. But, more importantly, some of these patterns would be quite difficult or impossible to mold unless they were mounted.

3/4" AC grade exterior glued plywood serves very well for mounting patterns. The details of mounting the patterns on the match-plate will be covered later. Figure 8 illustrates a match-plate pattern with a large disc pattern mounted on the COPE (upper) side and a small disc pattern mounted on the DRAG (lower) side. Notice the direction of draft both above and below the match-plate. The path for the molten metal to enter the mold is formed by the SPRUE and the GATES (OR RUNNERS). And note that the gates for the small disc overlap on both sides of the match-plate so that a continuous path is formed for the molten metal. Figure 9 illustrates the casting that results from molding the match-plate.

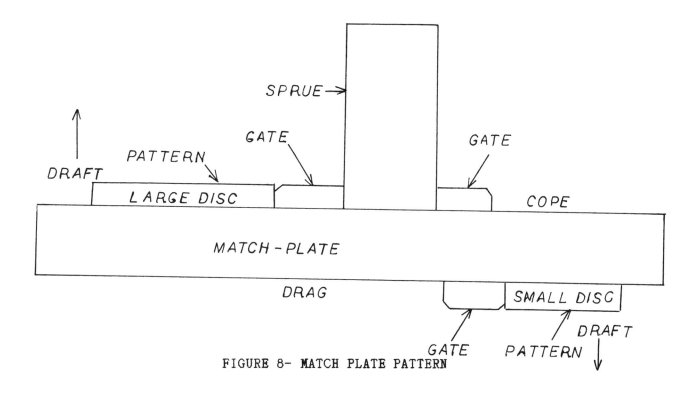

FIGURE 8- MATCH PLATE PATTERN

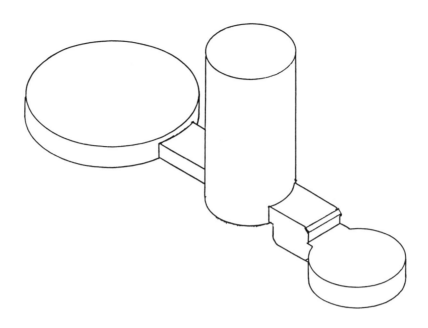

FIGURE 9- CASTING OF TWO DISCS

When finally finished one or two coats of varnish or paint will seal the
pattern against moisture penetration. Paint or varnish often raises the
grain of wood so it may be neccessary to sand some surfaces after drying.
Any remaining tips on producing the patterns will emerge as we discuss each
pattern individually.   And molding the patterns will be discussed
separately.

THE PARTS KEY

Before discussing the various individual patterns it will be well to become
familiar with the names of the parts.   Not all of these parts will be
castings but we will list all of them here before proceeding.

By examining the parts key in figure 10 and the top view in figure 11 you
will be better able to understand the relationship between the various
parts.   Notice that the air line adapter fittings are shown 90 degrees out
of postition in the parts key drawing.   This is done so that the transfer
piston rod will be visible in this drawing.   But the correct location is
shown in the top view and also in the individual detail drawings.   Notice
also that both the transfer cylinders and the power cylinders are offset by
1/8" so that the connecting rods can overlap on the crank pin.   See how the
power piston is a close fit in its cylinder but the transfer piston does
not contact the cyliner walls at all.   Of course the internal parts are the
same in the opposing pair of cylinders.   Details will be given in this
chapter for each pattern required.   Details for machining and finishing the
parts will be given in a later chapter.

The wooden stand should be hardwood and it will enhance the appearance of
the engine if it is nicely finished and varnished or painted.   It would be
well to prepare the stand first so it will be on hand when needed.

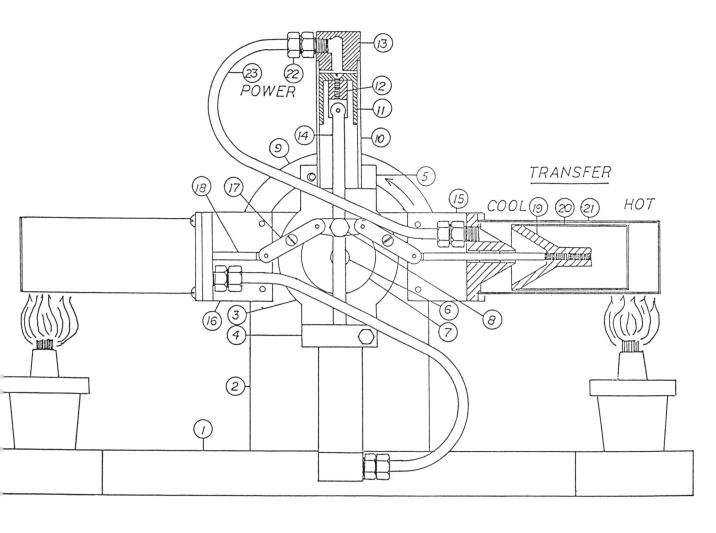

FIGURE 10- PARTS KEY

1-	WOODEN STAND	14- CONNECTING ROD
2-	BASE CASTING	15- RIGHT TRANSFER CYLINDER MOUNT
3-	POWER CYLINDER PLATE	16- LEFT TRANSFER CYLINDER MOUNT
4-	LOWER POWER CYLINDER MOUNT	17- TRANSFER PISTON ROD LINK
5-	UPPER POWER CYLINDER MOUNT	18- TRANSFER PISTON ROD
6-	CRANK PLATE	19- TRANSFER PISTON BASE
7-	CRANK SHAFT	20- TRANSFER PISTON
8-	CRANK PIN	21- TRANSFER CYLINDER
9-	FLYWHEEL	22- AIR LINE ADAPTER
10-	POWER CYLINDER	23- AIR LINE
11-	POWER PISTON	24- ALCOHOL LAMP
12-	GUDGEON & WRIST PIN	25- COOLING FINS
13-	POWER CYLINDER HEAD	

Some parts, such as small screws and bushings, are not numbered but will be
discussed later when they are made. The parts are listed and numbered in
the general order in which they will be made. More detailed drawings and
photos will appear when needed as the project progresses.

15

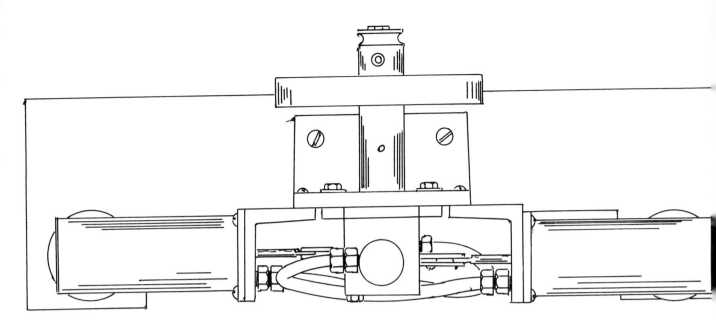

FIGURE 11- TOP VIEW

THE BASE CASTING PATTERN

Referring to figure 12, this pattern is most easily made up in three pieces
which can be finished to shape and dimension before assembling. Only a
side view and end view are given but every essential detail about the
bird's eye view can be gathered from what is shown so that you can form
that view in your mind's eye. Of course a view from below would show a
rectangle 3 1/16" wide and 4 3/32" long with the joint 5/16" from the end.
And the bird's eye view would be a rectangle of the same dimension but
showing the joints and fillets at the foot and the gusset. If you are not
accustomed to interpreting these ORTHOGRAPHIC views you should pause here
long enough to become comfortable with this portion of the craft.

Compare this pattern drawing with the drawing of the casting and you will
see where allowance has been made for shrinkage in length and width but
shrinkage has been ignored in the thickness and height of the members
because it is not significant in this instance.

Three degrees of draft has been allowed while one degree would actually be
adequate for a skilled molder. If you are a beginner you will appreciate
the advantage given by the extra draft and it will still be an acceptable
casting. In fact more draft could be allowed without a problem. Notice
that the arrow denoting "DRAFT" points upward in both views, which denotes
that all dimensions above the base line are smaller than the base line
dimension.

The larger rectangular portion is a uniform 1/4" thick while the foot and
gusset, which stand vertically during molding, are 5/16" thick at the base
line and 1/4" thick at the upper dimension. The upper dimensions are
approximate and not at all critical. But they are given to accent the
draft factor and to give something of a guide. The important thing is that
all vertical surfaces slope inward so that the pattern will easily withdraw
from the mold.

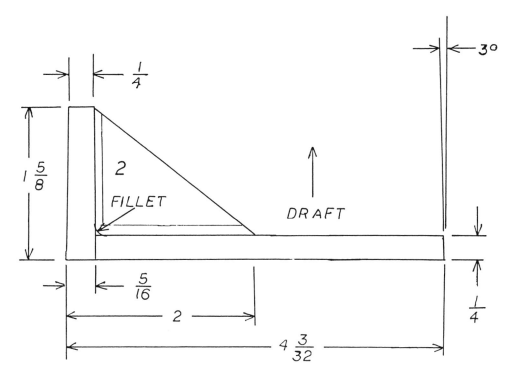

BASE CASTING PATTERN, SIDE VIEW

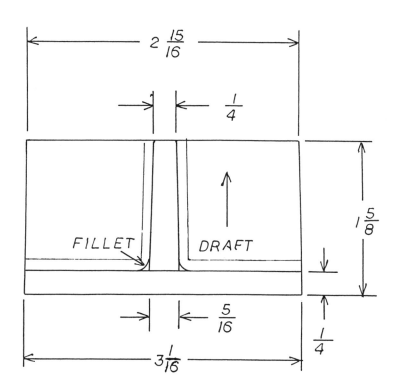

BASE CASTING PATTERN, TOP END VIEW

FIGURE 12

17

As you form the main rectangular part remember that the outside end and the two sides are drafted three degrees, which will be an acute angle from the base line. But the end that joins with the foot will be an obtuse angle. Also the angle between the horizontal and vertical edges of the gusset will be obtuse. Unless these members stand truly vertical the advantage of draft will be lost.

The only practical method of joining these thin sections is by gluing. To do that you must clamp the parts securely until the glue dries. It will be easy to improvise a wedge clamp on your bench top or a piece of plywood. Simply make a straight block and a tapered block of wood as shown in figure 13, and make a wedge to match the angle of the tapered block. Brad the straight block to the surface. Loosly assemble the pattern and brad the tapered block to the surface with the wedge aligning it. Then when you glue the joint and force the wedge in place the parts will be securely clamped. It may be neccessary to lightly brad the pattern to the surface if it tends to rise at the joint. You must also lay down a sheet of waxed paper or rub wax on the surface so that the assembly won't be glued to the surface when the glue oozes out of the joint upon clamping. The gusset can be bradded in place until the glue dries or brads can be permamnently left in the pattern. It will be best to pre-drill holes for the brads to avoid splitting the thin sections. You can simply cut the head from a brad and mount it in the drill chuck to drill starting holes. Make certain that the gusset and the foot member are truly vertical and that the pattern is well drafted on all sides.

When the glue has thoroughly set remove the wedge and use the angled block to finish-sand all of the vertical surfaces. Wipe a fillet on all inside corners and lightly round off all outside corners. Sand and scrape as required to produce smooth surfaces. Seal the pattern with varnish or paint and check for raised grain after the sealing coats dry.

When you have successfuly made this pattern you have actually mastered the major part of the pattern maker's craft. Other patterns will certainly be more intricate but you have applied all of the major principles in this exercise.

THE POWER CYLINDER PLATE PATTERN

This will be our first example of a match plate pattern but for now just make the parts and we will mount it with other patterns later. Like the base casting pattern, it will be easiest to make it in several pieces.

The challenge in match plate work is to achieve perfect register on both sides of the plate. That is: the portion of the pattern which is molded on the cope side must align perfectly with that on the drag side or a SHIFT will result in the casting. That would greatly increase finishing work and might possibly render it useless. The easy way is to drill a hole through the plate so that you have a precise reference on both sides. Since this pattern is symmetrical we can use the center member to both locate the pattern on the plate and to locate the sprue on the opposite side so that it will be accurately centered. In this instance the sprue will become part of the casting so its location, size and vertical alignment are critical.

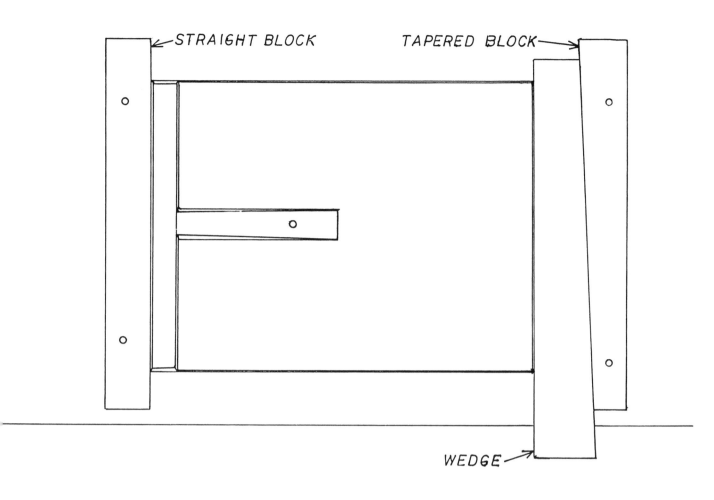

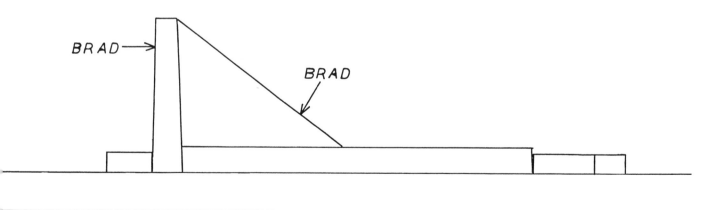

FIGURE 13- THE WEDGE CLAMP

19

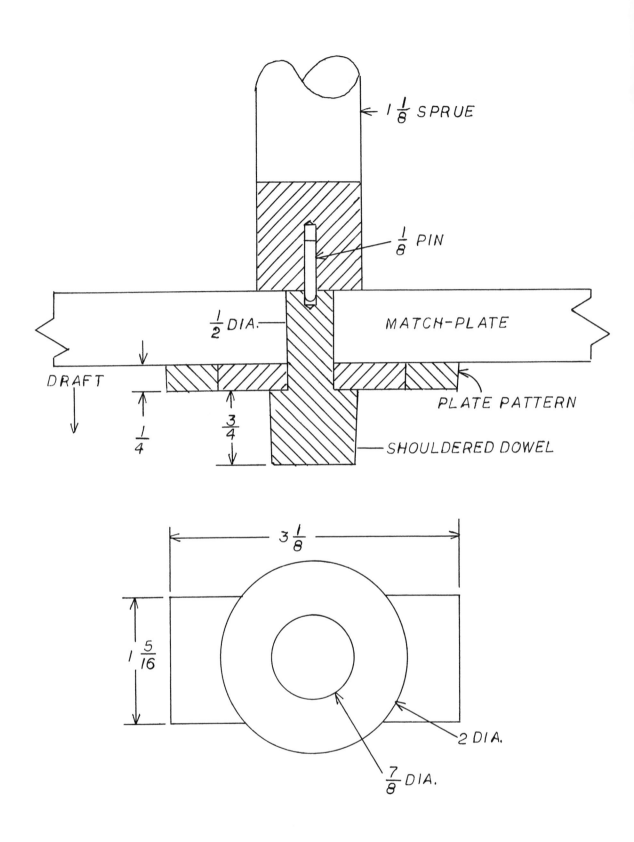

FIGURE 14- POWER CYLINDER PLATE PATTERN

So mount a piece of hardwood in the lathe chuck and turn a shouldered dowel
with the outer end 1/2" diameter and 1" long. Center drill the outer end
1/8" about 1/4" deep. Turn the inner end 7/8" diameter with three degrees
of draft and part it off at 3/4" from the shoulder. Note the direction of
draft in figure 14. The shouldered dowel will pass through the pattern and
the match plate and the 1/8" center hole will precisely align the sprue on
the cope side. The 3/4" length of the 7/8" diameter portion will seem to
be excess since it corresponds to the 3/16" X 3/4" diameter shoulder later
to be machined. But you will find that the extra length will be neccessary
to mount the casting for part of the machining operations.

The plate portion of the pattern could be jigsawed from a single piece but
that proves a tricky job when draft is involved. It is also difficult to
accurately center a 1/2" hole in such a piece. So I mounted an octagonal
piece of 1/4" thick stock on a 1/2" threaded arbor and turned it to 2"
diameter with three degrees of draft. Then I mounted a larger piece of
1/4" thick stock in the four jaw chuck and bored it for a close fit over
the 2" disc. And finally I cut the 1 5/16" wide end pieces from the bored
stock to form the ends of the plate. The pieces were drafted using the
angled blocks and then aligned and assembled with glue using the wedge
clamp method.

Later we'll drill a 1/2" hole through the match plate and mount the pattern
as shown in the sectional view in figure 14.

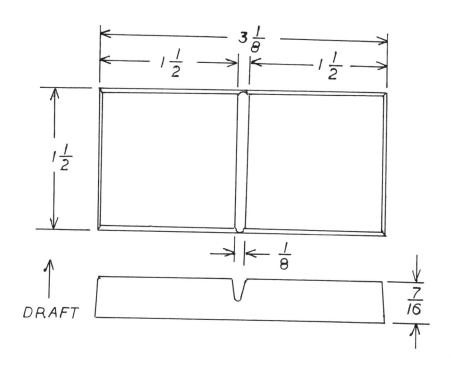

FIGURE 15- POWER CYLINDER MOUNT PATTERN

21

THE POWER CYLINDER MOUNT PATTERN

This will be the simplest pattern of all for it is merely a rectangle with
three degrees of draft on all four sides and a well drafted groove in the
center. The object is to cast rough flat stock from which we will machine
the rectangular brackets for mounting the power cylinders to the plate.
The groove will make it easy to cut the stock in half.   Dimension as
detailed in figure 15 for stock large enough for both mounts

THE FLYWHEEL PATTERN

It will be easiest to mount dressed 7/16" thick stock in the lathe on a
threaded mandrel to turn the main body of the flywheel as detailed in
figure 16.   Then turn the hub from stock mounted in the chuck and glue it
into the center hole of the main body.   The 1/8" center hole in the hub
will locate the sprue, which will have a pin centered in its end.

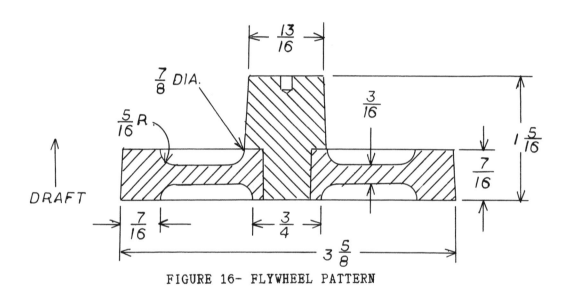

FIGURE 16- FLYWHEEL PATTERN

THE CONNECTING ROD PATTERNS

The connecting rods are the most delicate part in the project.   To carve
such a shape in wood requires considerable skill and they would be
extremely difficult to mold as loose patterns. But it is an easy matter to
accurately drill a pair of holes and glue in a couple of dowels.   Then the
body of the connecting rod is cut from 3/32" thick wood and glued in
between the dowels. The extension for the transfer piston rod link is also
glued in place. Note in figure 17 that the entire body is on only one side
of the match plate but the ends of the dowels protrude on both sides. One
dowel will be 5/16" diameter and the other will be 1/4". The length of the
dowels will be 5/32" longer than the thickness of the match-plate. They
will protrude just 1/32" on the cope side but 1/8" on the drag side. Thus
there will be a 1/32" boss on each side of the body. Notice also that the
extension for the transfer piston rod link is 3/32" thick like the body. A
few strokes with a file will easily reduce the thickness of the casting
later. Prepare two sets of pattern parts and they will later be mounted on
the match plate with other patterns.

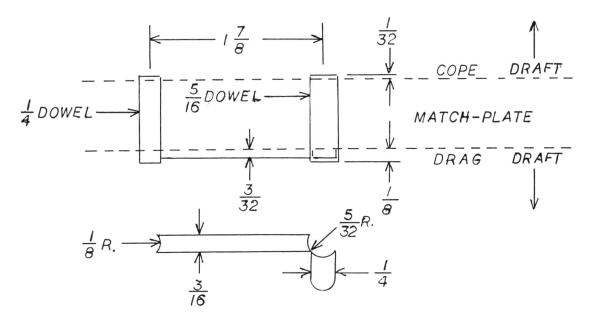

FIGURE 17- CONNECTING ROD PATTERNS

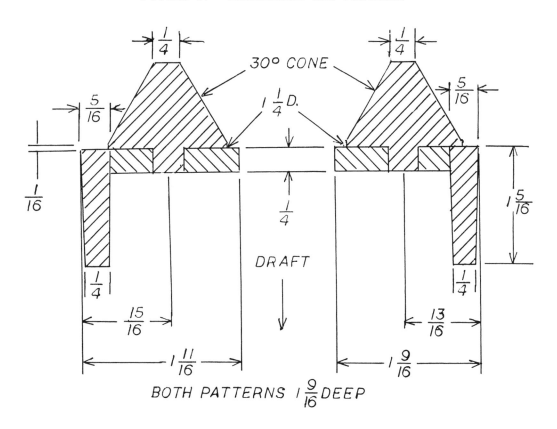

FIGURE 18- TRANSFER CYLINDER MOUNT PATTERNS

THE TRANSFER CYLINDER MOUNT PATTERNS

Figure 18 illustrates the profile of these two patterns. The cone portions
will easily be turned on the lathe and the bracket portion will best be
done in two pieces as was the base casting pattern. Again the wedge clamp

will make an easy job of gluing up the pieces. Notice that the horizontal part of the bracket is uniformly 1/4" thick while the vertical portion is tapered for draft. Of course all four sides of the bracket portion must be drafted. Both patterns will be 1 9/16" deep at the base line. Especially notice that there is a 1/8" difference in the center distances and the width. This will be important later when you machine these castings.

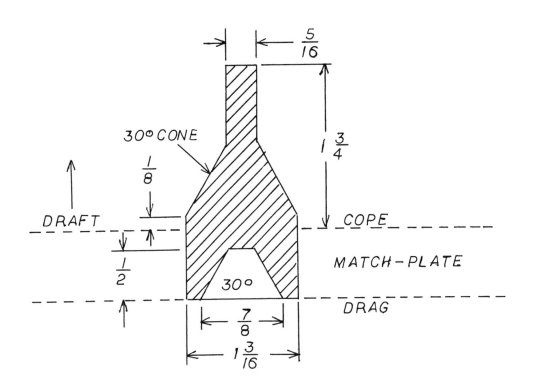

FIGURE 19- TRANSFER PISTON BASE PATTERN

THE TRANSFER PISTON BASE PATTERN

Upon first examination these match-plate pattern drawings may appear to lack important dimensions. But it is only the thickness of the plate that has been left out. The original patterns were mounted on 3/4" plywood but you may use a different dimension. Simply add the thickness of your plate for the total dimension of each pattern.

Figure 19 gives a clear profile of the transfer piston base. Two identical patterns will be required. The 5/16" diameter stem is made longer than required to provide a grip for machining the casting. Mount the stock in the lathe chuck and turn the major outside diameter and the inside cone first. With the same chucking turn the outside cone and finally the stem. Remember to give the stem a slight bit of draft and sand all very smooth before parting off.

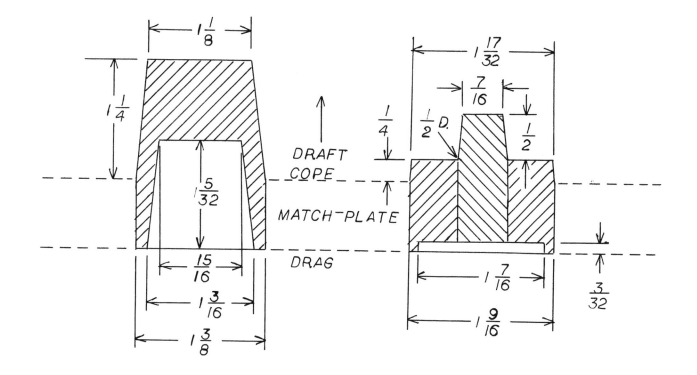

FIGURE 20- THE ALCOHOL LAMP PATTERNS

THE ALCOHOL LAMP PATTERNS

Figure 20 gives the profile view and dimensions. Two sets are required.
Like the transfer piston base, these patterns must be concentric so perform
all operations with the original chucking. For the reservoir turn the
outside diameter to the base line dimension. Then set the compound to 5
degrees to turn the outside taper and to bore the inside taper. Sand very
smooth inside and out before parting off.

While the cover pattern might be turned in a single piece it will be easier
to turn the outside diameter and then the shallow depression. Then center
drill and bore 1/2" through and part off. Finally, turn the 1/2" diameter
stem and glue it in place.

The overall length and the depth of the bores will be critical for that
will determine the thickness of the casting at bottom and top.

PREPARING TO MOLD THE PATTERNS

All that is required to achieve a successful foundry mold is to imbed the
pattern in the molding sand and then remove it without damaging the cavity.
A simple statement, but the deed is not always so simple. Some shapes are
unwieldy, to say the least. And others simply must be mounted upon a
broader surface in order to mold them at all. So several of these patterns
will be mounted and done in a single mold. These will be the power
cylinder plate, the connecting rods, the transfer piston bases and the
alcohol lamps together with their lids.

25

It would actually be possible to mount all of the patterns for this engine project on a single match-plate and shake all of the castings out of one mold. But such an intricate match-plate would really require a molding machine or at the very least some mechanical aid to ensure a perfectly straight lift when opening the mold and withdrawing the match-plate. So some of the patterns will be left unmounted. These are called LOOSE PATTERNS. The base casting, the flywheel and the power clinder mounts are easily molded as loose patterns.

The transfer cylinder mounts are in yet another classification because the cone portion interferes with laying them on the molding board for the initial operation. So we drill a pair of holes in the molding board for the cones to enter and then it becomes easy to mold these patterns just like any loose pattern. The drilled molding board is called a FOLLOW BOARD. We can make the board large enough so that the other loose patterns can be molded with the transfer cylinder mounts so only two molds will furnish a full set of castings for an engine.

THE MOLDING FLASKS

If you already have an assortment of flasks it will not be difficult to alter the layout of the match-plate and follow board to accomodate what you have on hand. But if you are setting up anew you will need two sizes of flasks: 8" X 12" and 10" X 12". Figure 21 illustrates the smaller flask. Of course larger flasks can be used or the layouts can be changed to use smaller flasks.

Common 1 X 4 stock is adequate and you can join the members with nails or screws. Glue will make a sturdier flask.

The brackets for the guide pegs are cut from 1" X 1/8" angle iron, about 2" long. The pegs are 1/4" X 4" bolts with the heads cut off. The brackets are fastened to the flasks with 1/4" bolts.

Common 1 X 4 stock is 3/4" thick and 3 1/2" wide. Add 3/4" to the nominal dimensions of the flask for the length of the sides. So four pieces 8 3/4" long and four pieces 12 3/4" long will make the cope and drag for an 8" X 12" flask.

The grooves can be cut with a router, dadoe head or multiple passes over the table-saw blade. If you clamp a wedge tapered about 2" per foot to the rip fence you can pass the stock over the table-saw blade at an angle to cut a semi-circular groove. Raise the blade no more than the depth of the saw-teeth at each pass .

Make the cross-cuts true square and assemble the flasks carefully so that they will meet well at the parting.

Make the guide peg brackets in matched pairs by clamping them together for drilling. Ream the holes slightly if neccessary to ensure that the pegs will slip in and out freely. However you want a mimimum of play to avoid shifting at the parting plane.

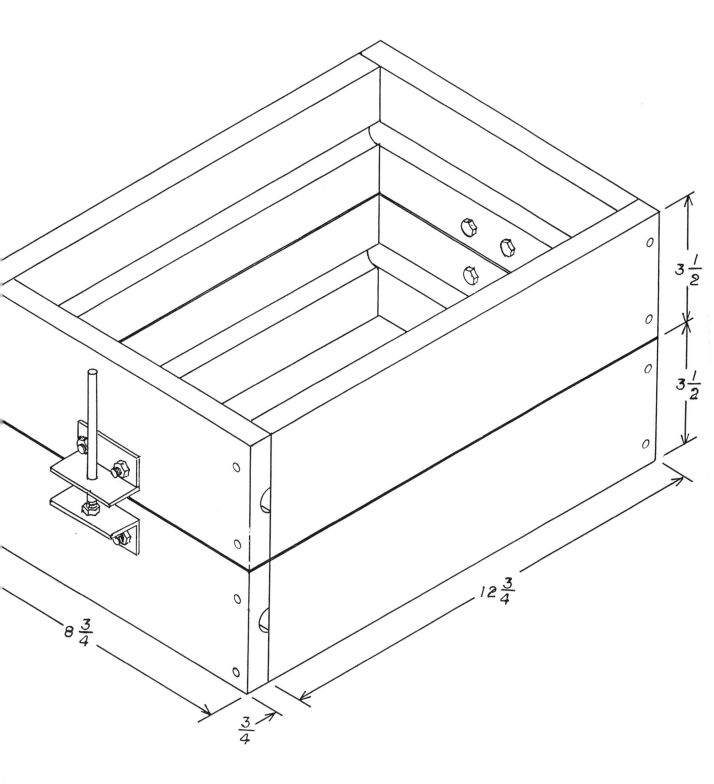

FIGURE 21- AN 8" X 12" MOLDING FLASK

Seal the finished flasks with varnish or paint so that they will not absorb
moisture.

THE MATCH-PLATE LAYOUT

The purpose of the match-plate is to secure the patterns in the proper position for molding and to enable you to rap the pattern to free it from the sand before the mold is opened. So the plate must be a bit larger than the outside dimensions of the flask and it must be rigid enough so that it won't yield under pressure of ramming up the mold. Of course it must also be of reasonably uniform thickness with both sides sanded smooth. 3/4" AC exterior glued plywood is ideal for the job. Make sure that the stock you select is truly flat so that it won't rock when laid on the flask.

The outside dimension of the 10" X 12" flask is 11 1/2" X 13 1/2". So prepare a match plate that measures about 12 1/2" X 15 1/2". Notches are cut in each end to clear the guide pegs.

Lay out and drill the match plate as detailed in figure 22. The prepared patterns for the transfer piston bases and the alcohol lamps will be installed in the circle of holes. A circular gate will feed the six radial runners. The power cylinder plate pattern and the connecting rod patterns will be joined together to be fed by a separate sprue.

The most practical way to drill the larger holes is with an adjustable hole-saw. The graduations on the common variety are not reliable enough for precise work so you must drill trial holes in scrap as you adjust to size. Make sure that the prepared patterns will slip easily into the trial holes before you drill the match-plate. A loose fit is OK for you can bed the patterns in the plate with polyester auto body putty, which will fill any gaps.

Notice in figure 22 that 5/16" notches are cut in each end of the plate to clear the guide pins on the flask. The outline of the flask is marked out as a reference and layout dimensions are made from the inside line.

Begin by marking out the center of the 4 1/2" circle upon which the six patterns will be located. Divide the circle into six equal spaces to locate the centers of each of the patterns. Then cut the holes for each of the patterns. Also layout and drill the 1/2" hole which will be the center of the power cylinder plate pattern and the 1/4" and 5/16" holes for the bosses of the connecting rod patterns.

Lay the plate on a flat surface with a sheet of waxed paper to avoid bonding the plate to the work surface. Coat each pattern with the polyester auto body putty and set them in their respective holes, making sure that they rest securely on the supporting surface so that the drag side will be even and the patterns will stand truly perpendicular. scrape away excess putty and make sure the patterns do not move until the putty has set firmly. Fill any voids with additional coats of putty and sand all smooth.

Prepare a disc 1 1/8" in diameter and 3/8" deep with a 1/8" center hole and glue it to the center of the circle. Split a 3/8" dowel and cut runners to fit between the disc and each pattern. Glue the runners in place.

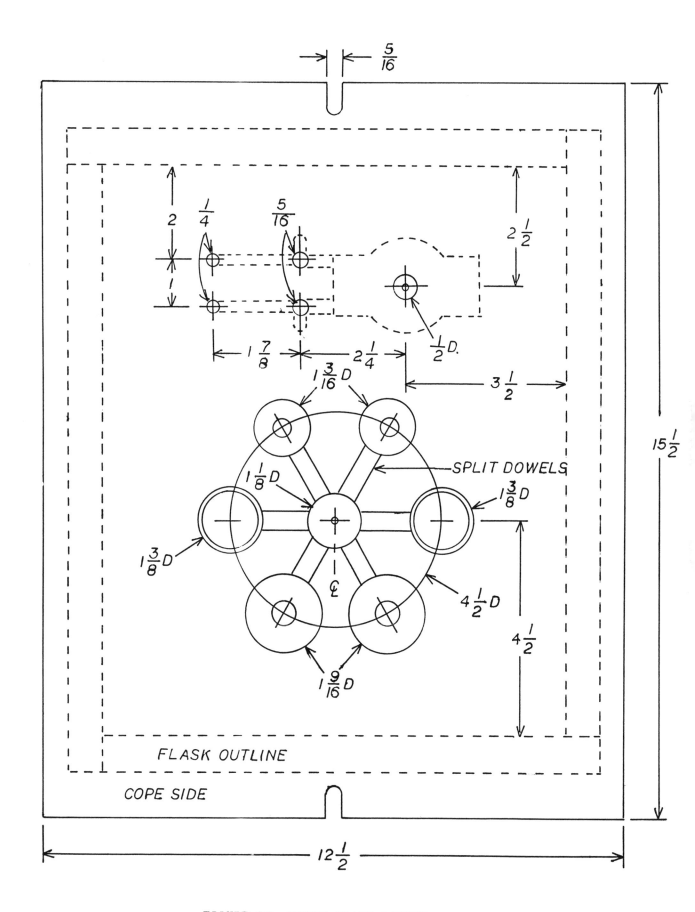

FIGURE 22- MATCH-PLATE LAYOUT

Note that the outlines of the power cylinder plate pattern and the connecting rod patterns are indicated with dotted lines. This means that they are installed on the drag side of the plate. Glue the power cylinder plate pattern in place with the shouldered dowel glued in the 1/2" hole. Glue the dowels that form the bosses of the connecting rod patterns into their respective holes with 1/32" protruding on the cope side of the plate. Glue the bodies and extensions of the connecting rod patterns to the drag side of the plate. Split a 5/16" dowel and prepare runners to feed the connecting rod patterns from the end of the power cylinder plate pattern. The ends of the runners that join to the rod bosses must be tapered and contoured to fit the bosses. Glue them in place to complete the match-plate.

When all surfaces are clean and smooth seal the match-plate with varnish or paint. Check for raised grain or any flaws after the sealing coat dries and correct as neccessary. Figure 23 is a clear view of the cope side of the finished match-plate. Of course the drag side will display the power cylinder plate pattern, the connecting rod patterns and the opposite details of those seen on the cope side.

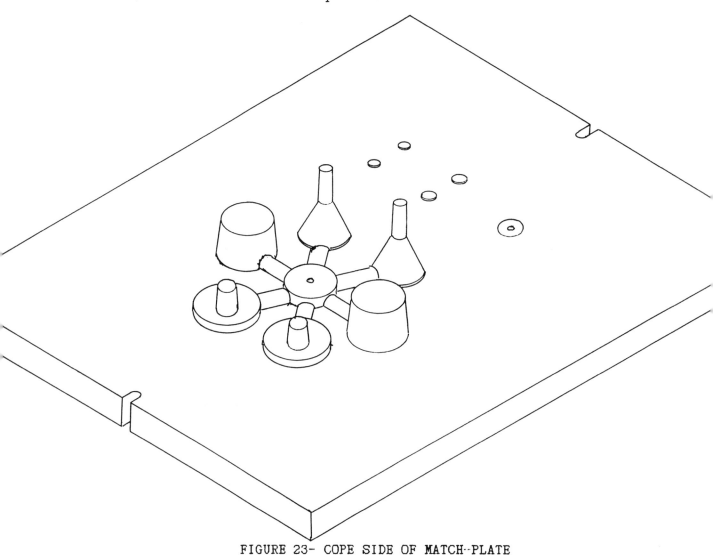

FIGURE 23- COPE SIDE OF MATCH-PLATE

PREPARE THE FOLLOW BOARD

The 8" X 12" flask will be adequate in size for the rest of the patterns. The follow board is prepared similar to the match-plate except that the patterns are not fastened to it permanently. And the follow board is not rapped before opening the mold so it need only be large enough to cover the flask. 10" X 14" will be adequate. In this instance it will serve as a follow board for the transfer cylinder mount patterns and a simple molding board for the remaining loose patterns.

Figure 24 tells the whole story. Simply bore two 1 1/4" holes to accept the cones of the transfer cylinder mounts. The flywheel, base casting and power cylinder mount patterns are layed on the board as indicated. All of the castings can be fed from the flywheel. The runners will be cut after the mold is opened and the patterns are removed.

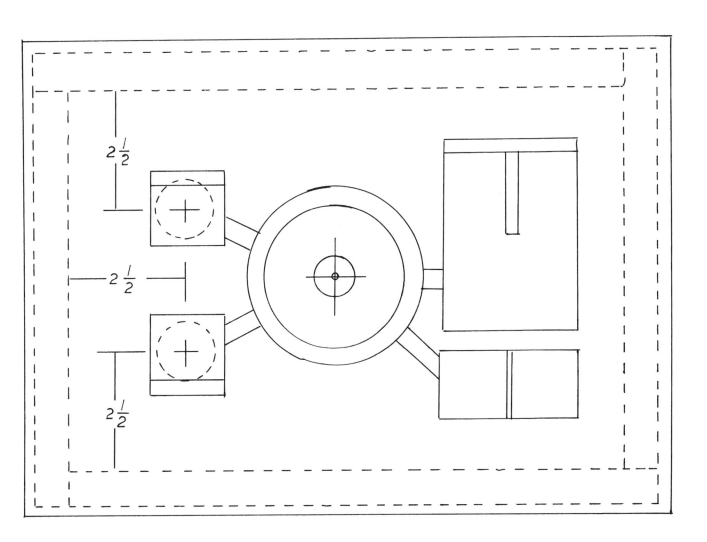

FIGURE 24- FOLLOW BOARD LAYOUT

Now that you have the patterns we can begin to prepare molds and produce castings. Figure 25 shows a full set of castings for one engine. Only the flywheel has been machined. The other castings appear in their rough condition. These castings are slightly different than detailed in this manual in some respects because the patterns have been modified.

FIGURE 25- A SET OF CASTINGS

FIGURE 26

Figure 26 shows some castings just as they are shaken from the mold. These were done on a match-plate similar to the one detailed in this manual. Note the large sprue in the center of the power cylinder plate and the runners that connect the other castings to it. In this case the transfer cylinder mounts were done with a match-plate but it proved quite difficult to lift the plate so a follow board was chosen instead.

Molding a match-plate differs only slightly from molding loose patterns. But it will require an extra measure of skill to open the mold and lift the match plate so do not be discouraged if your first few attempts do not turn out so well. Lifting the match-plate is really the same as withdrawing a loose pattern. It is done in a single, straight-up motion, which is an acquired skill like dancing. You just practice until you get it right.

Begin by setting the flask half with the guide pegs pointing upward. Set the match-plate on the flask with the cope side up and slide the other flask half onto the guide pegs. Invert the entire group, dust the match-plate with parting and proceed to ram up the drag. Press the sand very lightly into the alcohol lamp reservoirs with a finger but don't over-do it. If these cores are too firm they will not rap loose when you lift the plate. Also press the sand into other depressions amd corners with the fingers. Then proceed to ram up in the usual manner and finally strike off level and rub in a bottom board. Roll over the entire mold.

Notice that there is no connection between the two groups of patterns. So two sprues are required to pour the mold. A 3/4" sprue will adequately supply the circle of patterns, and the sprue will later furnish stock for turning the pistons. A 1 1/8" sprue pin supplies the remaining patterns and it becomes the shank of the power cylinder plate casting.

Set both sprue pins, dust with parting and proceed to ram up the cope. Again press the sand into close corners with the fingers first and then ram up and strike off in the usual manner. Remove the sprue pins and dress up the openings so that sand will not be washed into the mold when you pour.

With the rammer or a mallet, rap the plate on all four sides and all four corners. The idea is to free the patterns from the sand and slightly enlarge the cavities. Rapping also firms up the edges of the cavities.

Grasp the guide peg brackets firmly and lift the cope straight up in a single motion and set it on edge behind the drag. Of course if you allow the cope to tilt more than a degree or two parts of the mold will be broken away.

FIGURE 27- RAPPING THE MATCH-PLATE

FIGURE 28- LIFTING THE MATCH-PLATE

If the opening was successful you can prepare to lift the match-plate. Use the rammer or a light mallet to rap the patterns that will leave a core, especially the alcohol lamp reservoirs. The idea here is to rap straight down to ensure that the cores will break loose from the pattern and remain on the drag when you lift the plate. If you rap too hard from side to side the cores will shift and the walls of the castings will not be uniform.

Lift the match-plate with the same deft single motion you have mastered for opening the mold. It is worth the time and effort to acquire these skills. In the event of failures don't forget to check the patterns for rough spots.

Remember that hand molds are not as clean and perfect as machine molds and they do not have to be. When you get a pretty good mold go ahead and pour it. A coarse file will clean up the edges of a rough casting and the machining processes will catch the rest. It is most important to avoid sand inclusions in the castings so be especially careful to clean up the cavities, runners and sprues before you pour. And always turn the cope horizontal to dump out any inclusions before you swing it over the drag to close the mold.

Figure 29 shows a completed mold using the match-plate detailed in this manual. Note that the connecting rod cavities appear only in the drag half of the mold and that they are fed from the power cylinder plate cavity. Note also the smaller sprue in the circular cluster while the large sprue feeds the power cylinder plate. This match-plate is quite easily molded and easy to clean up.

FIGURE 29- A COMPLETED MOLD

It is rather difficult to vent a match-plate mold with the wire because the pattern elements are small and their location is difficult to remember after the mold is rammed up. In most instances venting with the wire will not be neccessary. But because of their very small size the connecting rods will need some help. You can perforate the mold with the wire near the end of each cavity after the match-plate is lifted. Perforate only the drag as it is laying on the bottom board. Never try to push the wire through the cope while it is standing on edge or you may break the mold.

Because of their thin section the connecting rods will tend to chill before the cavity is filled so make sure your melt is hot enough. And pour rapidly, keeping the sprue flooded all the while. Like most of the details of foundry work, this is an acquired judgement. It seems intimidating at first but it is a simple matter: If it solidifies before the cavity is filled it is too cold, venting is inadequate or you poured too slow.

The follow board is done in nearly the same way as the match-plate except that the board is not rapped before opening the mold. The transfer cylinder mount patterns are set in their holes and the other patterns are layed on the board as shown in figure 24. A 3/4" or 7/8" sprue pin is set in the center of the hub of the flywheel pattern.

Dust with parting and ram up the cope first. Strike off, remove the sprue pin and rub in a bottom board. Roll over the entire mold and lift off the drag half of the flask and the follow board. You will see all of the patterns imbedded in the cope with the cones of the transfer cylinder mounts protruding above the parting plane.

Dust the parting plane, set the drag half of the flask in place and ram up the drag in the usual manner. Strike off, rub in a bottom board and roll over the entire mold.

Lift off the cope and lay it on a bottom board to swab, rap and withdraw the patterns. Cut the runners as indicated in figure 24 and swab any areas that might wash away when you pour. Clean up as needed, especially at the sprue, and close up the mold for pouring. Again, turn the cope horizontal before swinging it over the drag so that any inclusions can drop free. And of course if the cope happens to drop out you will need only to make a new cope rather than an entire mold.

Be patient with yourself if you are newly acquiring these foundry skills. Remember that nothing but a little dust is lost when a mold does not turn out well. But you had that much more practice as you rammed it up and you will master it soon. It will be best to produce two or three sets of castings even if you plan to build only one engine. You might spoil one in the machining process or one might have an internal flaw. If you intend to produce a number of engines you should turn out all the castings you need and a couple extra sets to boot.

Now with a supply of castings on hand we can begin the machining operations.

CHAPTER II

MACHINING THE PARTS

Actually not all of the parts will be produced by machine-shop operations in the strictest sense, and the wooden stand is a case in point. But we will discuss each part in numbered sequence anyway. Special tooling will be presented as it becomes neccessary.

DETAIL 1- THE WOODEN STAND

Figure 30 gives all of the neccessary dimensions. So cut it from a piece of good hardwood stock and nicely sand all surfaces before sealing with stain and varnish or paint. It is a good idea to glue a square of felt on the underside at each end so that it won't mar a table or desk top when you demonstrate the engine to friends.

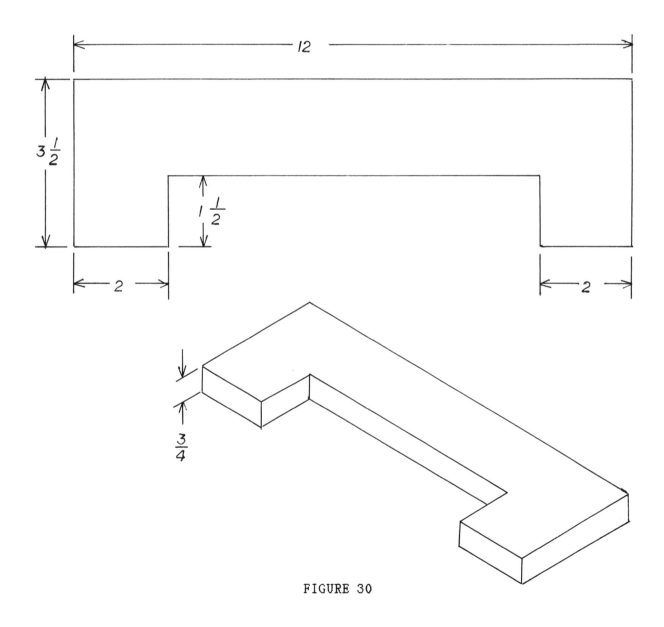

FIGURE 30

MAKE AN ANGLE PLATE

A number of operations to follow will require the use of an angle plate on the face plate. An expensive item to purchase. But you can easily make your own from aluminum castings for trifling cost.

Actually it requires an angle plate to make an angle plate on the lathe so you will have to make a pair of them. But they are such a valuable shop accessory that you will soon be glad to have at least a pair. The first step is to make a pattern and cast a pair in a size that will suit your lathe. The width should be about half the swing of the lathe but not less than 3 1/2". And the length should be three to four inches. 2" will be long enough to give adequate mounting surface for the foot.

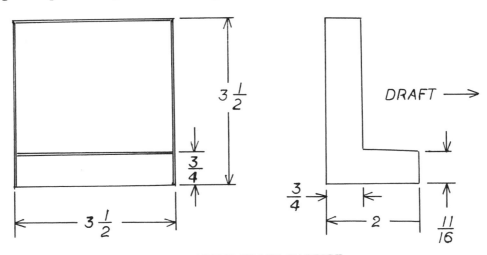

FIGURE 31- ANGLE PLATE PATTERN

Notice that the larger leg of the pattern is of uniform thickness while the smaller foot is drafted on the inside surface. The outside angle can be left very close to 90 degrees because such a simple pattern can easily be withdrawn from the mold at a slight angle. Easy to mold as a loose pattern. Cast two.

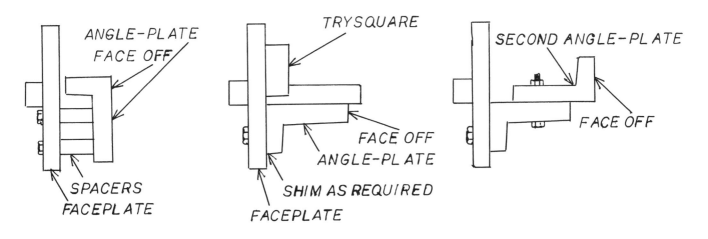

FIGURE 32- MACHINING SETUP

Drill and tap holes through the larger leg so that it can be bolted to the faceplate to face off the larger surface of the castings. Use spacers so that the short leg will clear and the machined surface will be parallel to the faceplate surface. Plan the hole location so that they can later be used to bolt both plates together while facing off the short leg. Face off the larger surface of both castings.

Drill and tap holes in the short legs to bolt the plates to the faceplate as shown in figure 32. Bolt one angle plate to the faceplate and shim as required to bring the larger surface to precisely 90 degrees as indicated with an accurate trysquare. This step determines the ultimate accuracy of both angle plates so be very fussy.

Bolt the second angle plate to the first as shown in figure 32 and face off the short leg. If the first plate is properly set up the outside angle of the second plate will be exactly 90 degrees.

Without separating the angle plates, invert the entire assembly on the faceplate. Since the base angle of the second plate has been faced off true there is no need for shims this time. Face off the short leg of the first angle plate. Both outside angles will now be identical.

Now you can carefully mount the angle plates to face off sides and ends so that you will have accurate reference surfaces for future setups.

These make a sturdy accessory for the shop and they will serve on lathe, miller, shaper, drill press or anywhere that the workpiece must be oriented at 90 degrees. Since they are cheap and easy to make you can consider them as SACRIFICIAL tooling. That is to say that you can drill and tap holes, cut grooves and notches or alter them in any way to accomodate a job. After many uses they may look like swiss cheeze so you simply melt them down and make a new pair.

MASS PRODUCTION

It is commonly believed that mass production is a phenomenon of our modern age and that it is a product of the industrial revolution. But even a casual study of history reveals that both medieval and primitive cultures have applied mass production methods to their industries. You can do it in your shop too. And it can be a very instructive and enjoyable experience. This engine project is ideal for a small mass production schedule because material costs are very low and equipment needs are quite basic. Even a very limited budget could afford to build several engines either to sell or to present as gifts. But for now it is suggested that you complete just one engine to become thoroughly familiar with all of the processes and operations. You will then be fully equipped and competent to produce as many as you choose cheaply and rapidly.

One essential element in mass production is SPECIALIZATION. In a large plant individuals concern themselves with only a narrow aspect of a product and so they become highly efficient. Of course any individual can become very skilled at many or all aspects, but at any given time will work at only one or two stations for greatest efficiency. For example a relief operator or foreman will take a station in an assembly line while regular operators take a break. So in your mini-plant you must be foreman or relief operator and master all operations. But you do them just one at a time. It is remarkably effective and it will enable you to turn out several engines in very short time. It is really no secret that knowledge results from study and skill results from practice. So merely understanding a process and doing it repeatedly will yield an expert in a short while. But keep in mind that careless work repeated over long periods of time is also practice, but it yields a bungling idiot. There is a stern discipline to mastering any craft.

A vital element in the success of a mass production operation is precision. No matter how rapidly or cheaply you turn out parts, they will be useless unless they fit properly. The speed results from using the same setup and tooling over and over again. But if the setup is not correct you merely turn out a big scrap heap. It was the concept of INTERCHANGEABLE PARTS production that gave the industrial revolution such momentum. For then it became possible to market everywhere in the world with assurance that repair or replacement parts shipped would fit perfectly. If the operation is functioning properly every part will be identical to the first. So you must test the first part to ensure that it fits as intended. The best test is the normal mating part or a gauge or fixture that exactly simulates the normal mating part.

In the limited home shop it will not be practical to produce all of the parts with interchangeable precision so some compromises must be made. In fact it is not practical to produce every part of most machines with such precision so some things are produced in assemblies that require some custom fitting of parts. For example you could not purchase a plunger for a hydraulic valve lifter on your automobile, but you could purchase the complete valve lifter as an assembly. That's because the plunger must be lapped to fit the barrel and tolerances are too close for interchangeable production. For the same reason you will have to hand lap or hone each power cylinder and then produce a piston to fit. So you will not be able to simply turn out a number of pistons to a given size. But you can gain the advantage of using many setups repeatedly, which will save much time and labor. And by producing the parts in groups you will save an amazing amount of time and labor. As each part is presented we'll discuss factors that determine special handling.

The all important factor in producing every part is the SEQUENCE OF OPERATIONS. In some instances doing the right thing at the wrong time will result in scrap. In other instances a number of diameters on a single part must be perfectly concentric so the part must remain in the chuck until all operations are complete. It is seldom possible to remove a piece from the chuck or faceplate and return it to its original setting. So you must make certain that your original setup will enable you to complete all of the required operations before you begin. And the setup must be secure enough to withstand the forces of applied tools without slipping or shifting. So we will sometimes be talking about doing a series of operations on one CHUCKING or one SETUP.

It is important to remember that each part bears a relationship with one or more other parts. You will have to make tests from time to time to ensure that what you are producing will function as intended. There are only two critical fits in the project, and that is the power piston to its cylinder and the transfer piston rod to its bushings. If these fit too loose or too tight the engine would run poorly if at all. There is not enough power to overcome excess friction and any air leak severely reduces power. Other important fit areas are the press fits of bushings and cylinder heads, the crank plate to crank shaft press fit and pivots at crank and wrist pin. A bit more discussion on fits as we progress.

With castings on hand and an angle plate on the face plate we can begin to produce the parts for the engine.

DETAIL 2- THE BASE CASTING

The first step will be to file away any flash at the edges and generally clean up the casting. A 16" double cut file is ideal for aluminum. A few passes of the file over the surface of the large leg will serve to clean it up. Only the small flange need be machined so that the vertical surface will stand truly perpendicular. This can be done on the miller or shaper if available. And it can even reasonably be done with the large coarse file though that might take considerable time and effort. But in most limited shops the most practical way will be with the angle plate on the lathe.

The two slots and the four small holes will be drilled later during assembly, using mating parts for templates. For now scribe horizontal and vertical center lines for the 7/8" hole that extend beyond the diameter of the hole for later reference. If a large swing lathe is available the 7/8" hole can be bored. A high speed hole saw was used on the original models and it was entirely satisfactory. Be certain to clamp the piece securely to the faceplate or drill press table for considerable force will be applied to cut, bore or drill such a large hole. This hole does not have to be precise since the shank of the power cylinder plate can be machined to fit.

The 7/8" hole can be used to mount the casting on the angle plate to face off the mounting flange. Then drill two 3/16" holes in the base flange for wood screws that will fasten it to the wooden stand.

Refer to figure 33 for all of the dimensions and details of the base casting. Since this is the first part to be produced all mating parts can be modified if neccessary so it is safe to produce as many as you wish.

Set the base casting aside for the present time. When the power cylinder plate and the transfer cylinder mounts are finished they will be used as templates to do the remaining work.

In a commercial mass production operation this is an area where a jig or fixture would be used to drill the remaining holes and mill the slots. But in a limited operation the cost and labor of producing the aids is not justified. However in a classroom project it would be well worthwhile to devise the neccessary simple tooling for the sake of the experience alone. A simple drilling template with hardened bushings and a fixture using the 7/8" diameter shoulder to position the work for milling the slots is all that would be required.

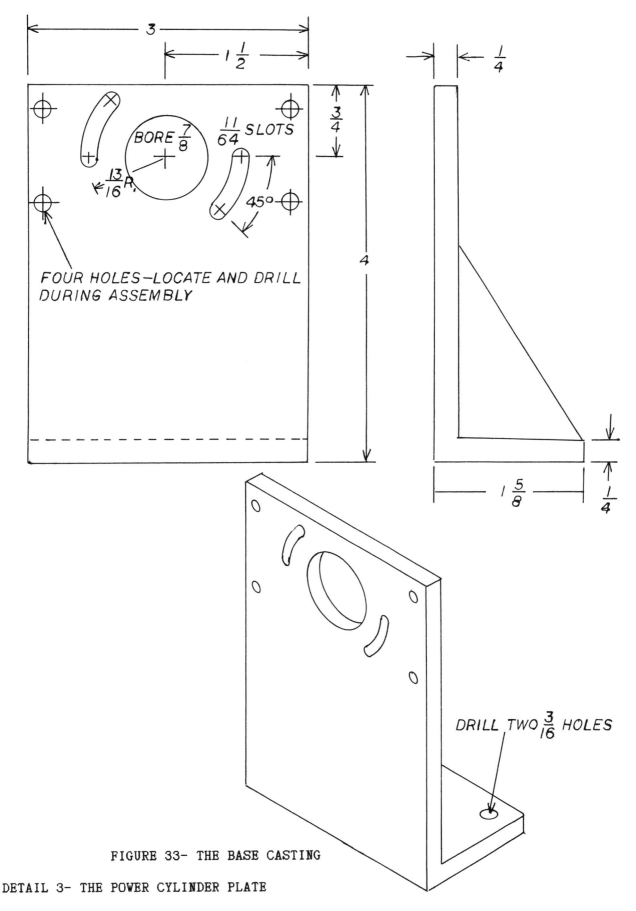

FIGURE 33- THE BASE CASTING

DETAIL 3- THE POWER CYLINDER PLATE

There are several lathe operations on this part and most of them must be done with one chucking so that they will be concentric. The equipment on

41

hand will determine the sequence of operations so study thoroughly before you make the first cut. And remember to match the actual diameter of the 7/8" diameter shoulder to the hole bored in the base casting. Make it .001" smaller for a close but free fit.

Notice in figure 34 that the long shank is 3/4" diameter with a 7/8" diameter shoulder adjacent to the plate. And the entire shank is bored through to 1/2" diameter. These three diameters are concentric so they are done without disturbing the setup in the chuck. And the back of the plate is also faced off in the same setup. After these operations are done the piece is reversed in the chuck to face off the front of the plate, part off the excess length of the short shank and face it off to leave the 3/4" diameter shoulder.

The casting has been designed with the short shank long enough so that it can be gripped in the lathe chuck to do the vital concentric operations and face off the back of the plate first. When these are done the piece is reversed in the chuck for the remaining work. Even if the chuck is out of true by several thousandths of an inch it will not matter since no other part mates with the outside diameter of the 3/4" shoulder.

Now the machined power cylinder plate can be used as a drilling guide to form the curved slots in the base casting.

First the two holes are drilled through the plate to tap size for 8-32 screws, which is a #29 drill size. A 9/64" drill is slightly larger than a #29 and would be acceptable in this instance. Do not tap the holes until the holes have been drilled in the base casting.

SLOTTING THE BASE CASTING

Clamp the base casting in the drilling vise with the power cylinder plate clamped in position. Use the drill press to drill tap size holes in a close series to form the curved slots in the base casting. These holes will be enlarged to 11/64" later so do not drill so closely so as to break out to adjacent holes or the work will be ragged and you may damage the plate.

The holes in the base casting are enlarged to 11/64" and the curved slots are then finished with a small file.

The holes in the power cylinder plate are tapped 8-32. The remaining four holes will be drilled later, using the power cyliner mounts as a guide.

Of course the curved slots can be quickly and easily done with an end mill if one is available. And precise jigs can be devised for every drilling operation.

THE CRANKSHAFT BUSHINGS

These are standard 1/2" X 3/8" oilite bronze bushings which can be purchased in many hardware stores or farm supply stores. Usually about 1 1/2" long so you can cut one in half to get two short ones. Chamfer the cut ends to remove burrs. Press the bushings into the bore and run a 1/2" reamer through if neccessary. The shaft must run very freely. Friction is a vital factor so we avoid a full length bearing here. A 1/16" oil hole in the shank will supply the reservoir between the two bushings.

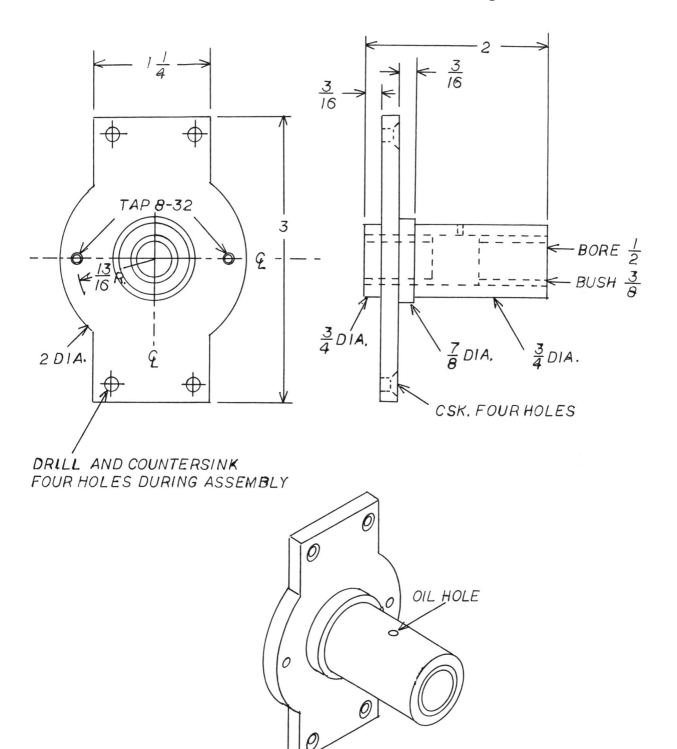

FIGURE 34- THE POWER CYLINDER PLATE

DETAILS 4 and 5- THE POWER CYLINDER MOUNTS

These are rather simple in appearance but rectangular shapes are a
challenge using only a lathe that seems oriented only towards producing
round or cylindrical objects. Naturally the job would be much easier if
3/8" thick bar stock was available. But that will not be the case in most
shops.

The critical dimension is the distance from the mounting surface to the
center of the bore. And of course the small holes for the mounting screws
and clamp screw are also tricky. A drilling vise is vital for this and
many of the drilling operations in this project. These will be used as a
guide to drill the remaining four countersunk holes in the power cylinder
plate so there is a drilling sequence.

If you are using the rough castings detailed in this manual they will first
have to be Squared up and sized on the lathe, shaper or miller. A number
of rough castings can be clamped in the four jaw chuck on the lathe or in
the vise of shaper or miller. Notice that both mounts are 1 1/4" wide but
there is a 1/8" difference in height. There is also a 1/8" difference in
the center height of the bores.

When they are squared and sized the location of the bore center can be
marked and punched. A wiggler, indicator or the tail center can be used to
center them in the four jaw chuck for boring. Make certain that they are
clamped radially true so that the bore will be parallel to the mounting
surface. Drill a starting hole with the tailstock chuck and bore to .750".

Next the tap sized hole for 8-32 screw is drilled all the way through on
one side of the bore. Do not drill the second shallow hole at this time.
Use a drilling vise with the drill press to ensure that the through hole is
truly perpendicular and well centered.

Cut the slit at the center height of the hole with a hacksaw or slit it in
the miller. Slip a scrap of sheet metal in the slit and enlarge the upper
half of the through hole to 11/64".

Use the upper hole to guide the tap to cut 8-32 threads through the lower
half of the hole.

You can now mount it on a 3/4" arbor to face off both sides to finished
thickness. The mounts are ready to be used to finish the power cylinder
mounting assembly.

THE POWER CYLINDER MOUNTING ASSEMBLY

Locate and drill two 11/64" holes in diagonally opposite corners of the
power cylinder plate so that the mounts will be positioned as shown in
figure 35. Countersink the holes so that flat head machine screws will be
slightly below the back surface.

Install the mounts with one 8-32 X 1/2" machine screw each and align them
so that they are parallel. Now you can safely locate the second hole.
Drill #29, tap the mount and enlarge and countersink the hole in the plate.

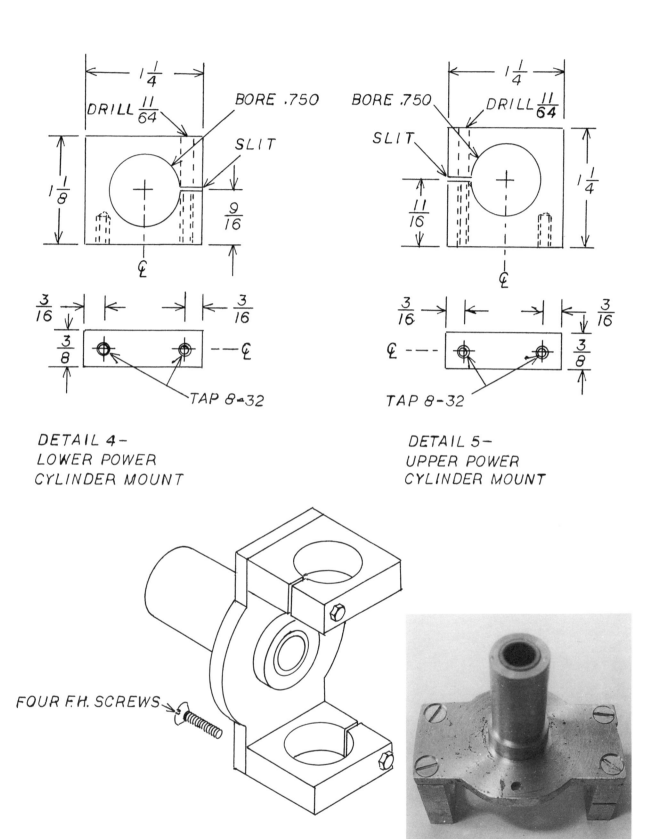

DETAIL 4–
LOWER POWER
CYLINDER MOUNT

DETAIL 5–
UPPER POWER
CYLINDER MOUNT

FIGURE 35- POWER CYLINDER MOUNTING ASSEMBLY

45

THE CRANKSHAFT ASSEMBLY

The shaft itself is simply a 3 1/2" length of 3/8" drill rod or mild steel shafting with a shoulder turned for a press fit in a 5/16" hole in the plate. The plate can be a scrap of 1/4" thick mild steel cut to octagon shape and pressed onto the shoulder to turn it round and face off to thickness.

It is best to drill the hole in the plate under size and ream to 5/16". It is always easier to prepare a shaft to fit a hole than it is to prepare a hole to fit a shaft.

When the plate is turned to size and faced off on both sides clamp it in the drilling vise to drill and tap the 8-32 hole so that it is parallel to the shaft.

Refer to figure 36 for details and dimensions.

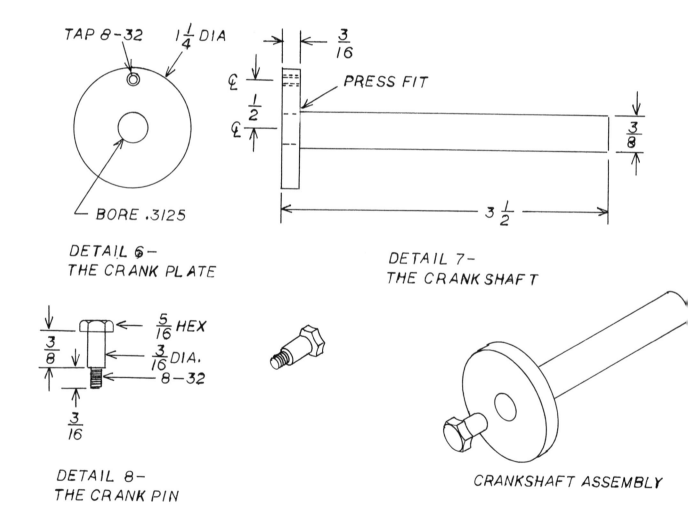

FIGURE 36- THE CRANK SHAFT

THE CRANK PIN

At first glance this little part is intimidating to the beginner but it is
really very easy to make. Dimensions are shown in figure 36.

Certainly if you choose you could simply turn the blank to dimension as
shown in the drawing, thread it with a die and part off to leave a round
head which you could finish with a screwdriver slot. But it will be much
more fun to finish with a hex head.

It will require some simple tooling which will improve your bench grinder.
It will also enable you to make some other hex head screws needed for this
project and for any future projects.

TOOLING FOR HEX HEAD SCREWS

It will be simple to chuck a piece of drill rod or mild steel and turn the
diameters for thread, shoulder and head as shown in figure 37.   Then
thread, part off and finish the head.

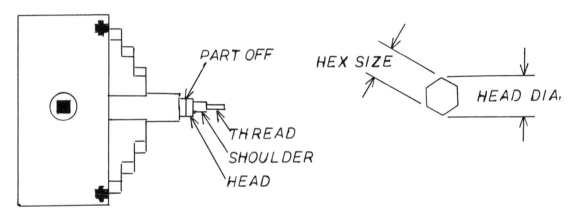

FIGURE 37

It is not practical to cut such fine threads on so delicate a piece with
the lathe's threading mechanism.   What is needed here is a tailstock die
holder to hold the die radially true as it cuts the threads.   Such a tool
can be made quickly and easily with some standard set screw collars and
some bits of mild steel rod and a spring that might be found in the junk
box. Refer to figure 38 for a general view of the tool.

Begin with a 3" length of 3/4" mild steel round and turn a .627" shoulder
1/2" long on one end. Remove the set screw from a 5/8" collar and press it
onto the shoulder. Bore or ream a 3/8" hole through the shaft and turn a
1.002" shoulder on the 5/8" collar.   Remove the set screw from the 1"
collar and drill and tap an 8-32 hole centered 3/16" from the edge. Press
the 1" collar onto the shoulder of the 5/8" collar. Prepare a 3" length of
3/8" shaft with a 60 degree center to fit the bore of the 3/4" shaft. Lock
the 3/8" collar near the centered end and install it with the spring to
complete the tool. This arrangement will provide a socket for a standard
1" die which will be locked by the 8-32 screw. The spring pressure feeds
as the work is turned by one hand while the other holds the tool.

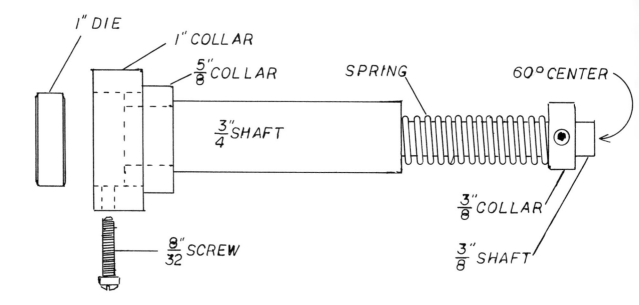

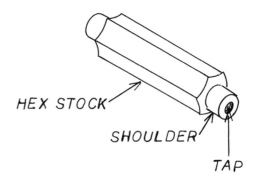

FIGURE 38- TAILSTOCK DIE HOLDER

If you want a hex head simply measure across two opposite points to find the diameter of the blank you need. Then we need an indexing fixture and a means to form the hex. Lacking the conventional milling and indexing equipment, you can easily adapt your bench grinder to do the work.

The indexing device is a short length of hex stock that is center drilled and tapped to accept the screw thread as in figure 39. The hex stock can be any size that is larger than the head you expect to make. Just mount it in the three jaw chuck to drill and tap it. And turn a shoulder so that the holder will clear the grinding wheel. You can prepare each end for a different size.

FIGURE 39- INDEX/HOLDER

The only modification to the bench grinder is to add a plate and guide to the tool rest as shown in figure 40. This not only provides a convenient work table for the index/holder, but also is useful for other grinding jobs. The size is not critical and will vary according to the size and design of your grinder. The slot in the plate enables you to adjust the guide for the depth of cut.

Note that the arrangement uses the right hand side of the grinding wheel so that the friction applied to the head of the screw tends to tighten it in the holder.

The prepared blank is screwed into the index/holder and the round head is applied to the grinding wheel with the guide limiting the depth of cut.

The depth of cut is discovered by trial on the first screw. All six facets are ground and then the hex is checked using a socket or nut driver as a gauge. When the correct setting is found you can produce many identical screw heads rapidly.

Of course the work must be cooled in water. It goes without saying that eye protection must be worn. And every grinding wheel must have a guard. All wheel manufacturers advise against using the side of the wheel as we are doing here. But this is very light work and it should not strain a sound wheel. Nevertheless, do not stand in line with the wheel while grinding in case it should break.

The convenient hex size for the crank pin is 5/16", and 1/4" seemed ideal for the 8-32 screws used on the power cylinder mounts and the clamp screws for the power cylinder plate. .290" diameter provides enough stock to form a 1/4" hex and .360" is OK for 5/16" hex.

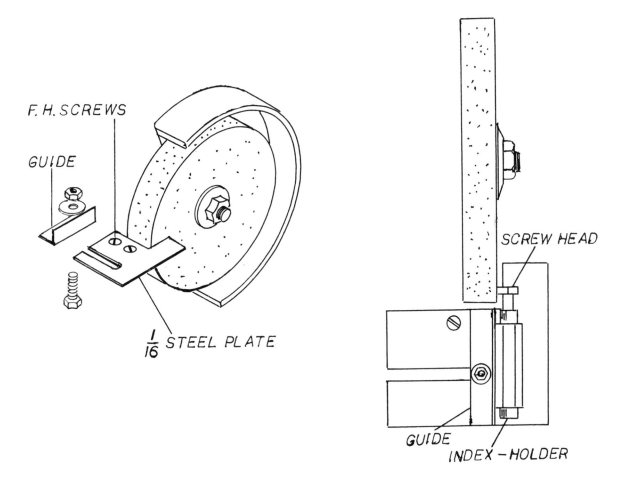

FIGURE 40- HEX GRINDING SETUP

Although slotted screws can be used to clamp the power cylinder mounts hex head screws will be better. The flywheel will make the screws that clamp the plate to the base inaccessible with a screwdriver so hex head screws are preferred in that location too.

49

DETAIL 9- THE FLYWHEEL

All of the dimensional detail for the flywheel is found in figure 41. The usual procedure would be to mount it as well centered as possible to bore the hub. It's best to bore to near size and finish with a reamer. Then install the set screw and mount it on an arbor to true up the outside diameter and turn the long hub and pulley groove. The amount of facing off on the sides will depend upon the quality of the casting and your preference.

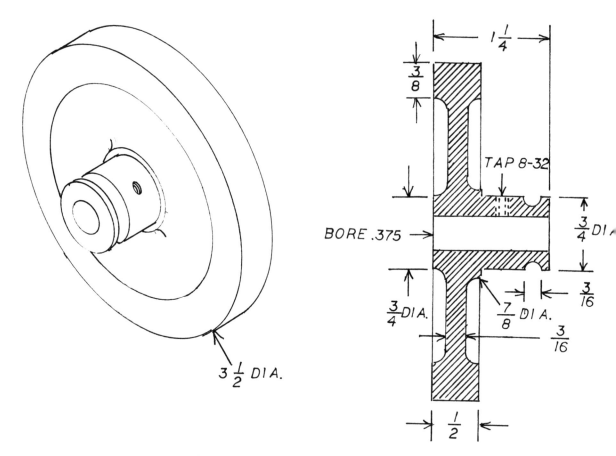

FIGURE 41- THE FLYWHEEL

THE CYLINDER LAP

Lathes do not bore perfectly round holes and there is certain to be a significant amount of taper in most instances. And the best of tool finish would not be acceptable for the power cylinder bore. So we must finish by honing or lapping and this work is best done before the piston is made. Not many home shops have access to a pin hone so you will probably have to make a lap.

A lap is an abrasive charged tool that is applied to the work. It can be made for inside or outside work and in any practical shape. It is made of material that is softer than the workpiece so that the abrasive grains will not be imbedded in the workpiece. Laps are commonly made of castiron,

50

copper, lead and even hardwood. Lead is probably the most practical choice for the limited shop.

It will be easy to mold and pour some 3/4" lead turning stock to make the laps. They are expendable so be prepared to make new ones from time to time.

Dimensional details are shown in figure 42. Prepare the mandrel first by turning a 1/4" X 3/8" long shoulder on the 3/8" X 4" mild steel shaft. Thread the shoulder 1/4"-20. Cut a lap blank to length, center drill it 1/2" deep and tap 1/4"-20. Screw the blank onto the mandrel, chuck it in the lathe and turn it to shape and dimension. Since the cylinder is gradually enlarged the lap must be adjustable. So we cut a slot with the hacksaw and install a headless screw to expand it as needed. The 1/8" hole at the end of the slot helps to prevent breaking.

In use the lap is charged with abrasive compound by spreading a small dab of compound on a flat hard surface and rolling the lap through it. The particles of abrasive imbed in the soft lead.

Chuck the mandrel in the drill press to drive the lap at moderate speed. A small can of kerosene on the drill press table will catch the drippings as you flush the work by dripping the kerosene through the cylinder with a small paint brush. The work is kept in vertical motion all the while to prevent RINGING, which is a deep groove in one place. The lap is not permitted to go more than 1/8" beyond either end of the cylinder to avoid BELL-MOUTHING, which means a widening of the ends of the bore.

The power cylinder mounting assembly provides an ideal fixture to hold the cylinders for lapping. The lap is expanded to give light to moderate resistance at the smallest area of the cylinder. When beginning you will feel more resistance in some areas. So you continue to lap until those high areas are cut away and then expand the lap a bit more. In time the resistance will feel uniform from one end to the other and you will then know that the bore is parallel. Then you continue to lap until a visual inspection reveals a uniform texture from end to end. The object is to produce a cylinder that is truly round with parallel walls. It will be neccessary to recharge the lap from time to time. It is the abrasive that is imbedded in the lap that does the work so don't waste the stuff by putting gobs of it in the cylinder. When the work is finished flush the cylinder thoroughly to remove all traces of abrasive.

The ultimate finish will depend somewhat on the condition of the bore when you begin. Lapping is a slow process and it can take hours to increase the size of a bore a few thousandths of an inch. Tiny flaws or a slight ripple will not seriously effect the operation of the engine. But any flaw that extends the length of the bore will surely mean a serious air leak.

Abrasive compounds are increasingly difficult to find in many areas. You may be able to find valve grinding compound at a local auto supply store, and it will work OK. 2 ounce cans of compound are available from Campbell Tools Co., 2100 Selma Road, Springfield, Ohio 45505, and from Power Model Supply Co., Rte 1, Box 177, DeSoto, MO 63020. 120 coarse grit will serve your needs for this project.

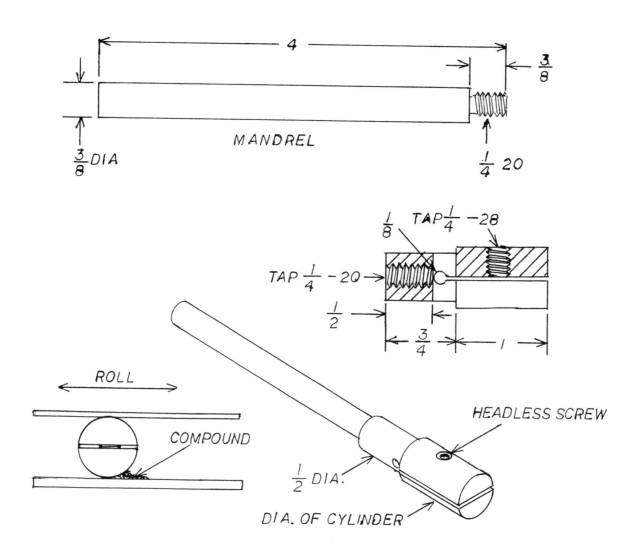

FIGURE 42- THE CYLINDER LAP

DETAIL 10- THE POWER CYLINDER

Mount a 3" length of standard 1/2" pipe in the chuck well centered. Since both inside and outside will be machined there is no point in using galvanized pipe unless you just happen to have it on hand. Used pipe will be OK if it is clean. But used pipe from some applications may become work hardened or effected by materials it carried. It will be difficult to produce a clean straight bore if there are hard spots.

If it is well centered in the chuck standard weight 1/2" pipe will clean up nicely when bored to .650". That is only .025" larger than 5/8" and that is not enough difference to effect the ratio between the transfer and power cylinder size. On the first two or three passes with the boring bar the seam is cut away and then it is smooth boring. Use the stoutest boring bar you have with a minimum of overhang. Use your finest feed on the last two passes for a minimum of lapping later. Turn the outside diameter to .750 after the bore is finished. Face off the outside end and chamfer slightly inside and out. Part off to length and deburr the parted end.

52

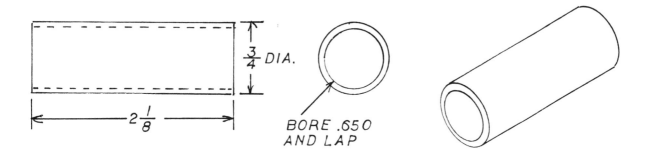

FIGURE 43- THE POWER CYLINDER

DETAIL 11- THE POWER PISTON

Refer to figure 44 for all of the dimensional detail. The pistons can be made of aluminum bar stock or from a length of sprue. They can also be made of brass if you happen to have some bar stock on hand.

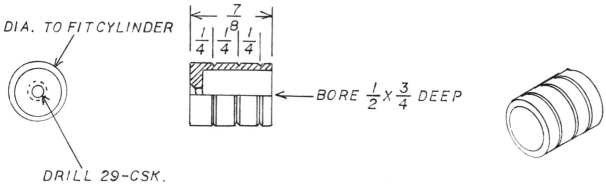

FIGURE 44- THE POWER PISTON

The outside diameter requires considerable caution since the piston must be a very close but frictionless fit in the cylinder. Most home shops will not have small hole gauges and it is a tricky business to measure such a small bore with vernier calipers. A practical method is to make a GO-NO-GO gauge. Just chuck a length of aluminum sprue and turn a shoulder about 1/4" long that will slip into the lapped cylinder. Then turn another short shoulder adjacent to it that is .001" larger. If the second shoulder will still slip into the cylinder turn another adjacent to it and .001" larger. Continue until you reach a diameter that will not slip into the bore. The preceding shoulder will be very near to the correct size. Make sure that the end of the cylinder is chamfered and that there are no burrs to interfere with the fit. When you are certain that the gauge fits properly you can measure it to discover the required outside diameter for the piston. And the cylinder itself will serve as a gauge to test the piston as you finish its outside diameter.

It will be an easy job to chuck the stock, face off the end and bore 1/2" diameter 3/4" deep. Use the center drill in the tailstock chuck to start the #29 hole to ensure that it does not run off. The hole will be countersunk after parting off. Then proceed to turn the outside diameter, testing with the cylinder as you near final size. Finally, use a threading tool bit on the tool post to cut the three grooves. Part off at 7/8" length and chamfer before the parting is complete. Countersink the hole in the top of the piston so that the 6-32 screw head will be flush.

The final test of the piston is made when the gudgeon is installed. Then it should remain at the top of the cylinder when the bottom is closed with a finger, and fall freely of its own weight when the air is allowed to escape. This test is made with both piston and cylinder dry. Both piston and cylinder must be absolutely free of dirt oil or dust. If the fit proves too tight you can prepare a short spindle with a 6-32 tapped hole in the end and screw the piston to it to take a light cut with a file. Don't finish the piston with abrasive cloth or some of the grains may imbed in it and spoil the cylinder.

DETAIL 12- THE GUDGEON AND WRIST PIN

I tried to find a different name for this thing, but the word means pivot or journal and that is exactly what it is so I gave up. It provides the pivot for the connecting rod and makes for very easy assembly. The wrist pin is merely a 3/8" length of 1/16" drill rod that floats freely in the gudgeon. The walls of the piston prevent its moving sideways enough to leave its bearing. Dimensional details are in figure 45.

Just chuck a piece of brass rod and turn the outside diameter. Face off the end, center and drill a #33 hole and tap it 6-32. Part off at 5/8" length. It can be screwed to a scrap of angle iron to clamp it in the vise for cutting the 1/8" slot, which can be done with hacksaw and file or a miller. The same angle iron fixture can be used to drill the 1/16" wrist pin hole.

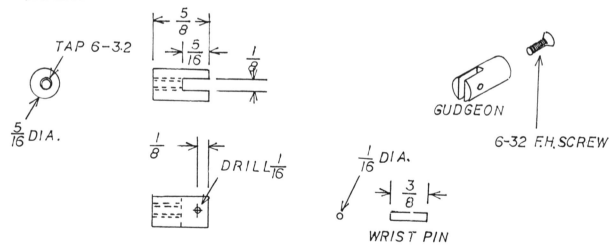

FIGURE 45- THE GUDGEON AND WRIST PIN

The important thing is to have the end of the gudgeon faced off squarely so that it will mount truly parallel to the piston's skirt. And the wrist pin hole must be exactly perpendicular to the axis of the gudgeon so that it won't bind the connecting rod.

54

Now the gudgeon can be installed in the piston so that you can test the fit in the lapped bore. A #6-32 flat head screw about 5/16" long is required to install the gudgeon. A very handy tool for shortening small machine screws is the crimping tool for solderless electrical terminals. The screw is simply threaded into the plate and a squeeze of the handle cuts it off to length without damaging the threads. It is likely that you will have to cut off a number of machine screws for this project.

FIGURE 46- CRIMPING TOOL

DETAIL 13- THE POWER CYLINDER HEAD

This one is quite simple and all of the details are in figure 47. It can be made of mild steel, aluminum or brass and the only critical fit is the shoulder that presses into the power cylinder. I made my first set of steel and brazed them in. But that is a demanding chore and I was pleased when Ben Imbrock of Anadarko, Oklahoma pressed his in with thread lock compound as a sealer and it proved entirely satisfactory. I made my second set of steel and pressed them in with thread lock and it worked fine.

So just turn the shoulder to .001" over the size of the lapped bore. Turn the outside diameter to 3/4". Drill the 3/16" hole 5/8" deep and part off at 11/16" length. Clamp in the drilling vise and drill the side hole #3 or 7/32". Tap the side hole 1/4"-28 and press the head into the top of the cylinder with thread locking compound.

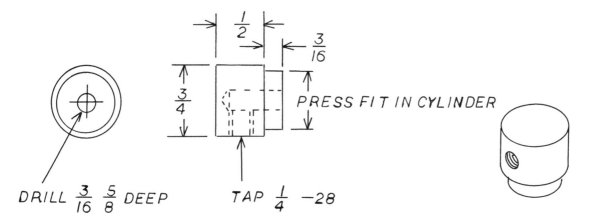

FIGURE 47- THE POWER CYLINDER HEAD

DETAIL 14- THE CONNECTING ROD

Probably the most delicate part in the project but it will be easy if you prepare a small hardwood block to support it while drilling and filing. You will have to locate the holes precisely and thin the bosses at both ends, and also thin the arm that connects to the link.

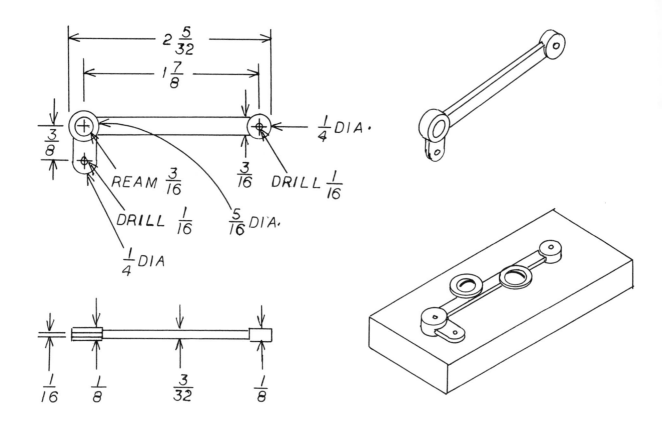

FIGURE 48- THE CONNECTING ROD

Refer to figure 48 for details and prepare the small hardwood block with slight depressions to accept the bosses at each end. This will enable you to rest the casting firmly while you drill it. You can use a couple of small screws with washers to clamp the casting down temporarily.

Very carefully mark the hole centers and drill three 1/16" holes through the casting and into the hardwod block. Cut two pins from 1/16" drill rod and push them through the holes in the two bosses and into the block so that they are flush with the surface of the bosses.

Now you can remove the clamping screws and put the block in the bench vise to file the first side of the bosses and reduce the first side of the link arm.

You may also want to thin the web a bit at this time. Then lift it off the pins and turn it over and press it onto the pins again to do the reverse side.

Enlarge the hole in the lower boss by steps and finish with a 3/16" reamer. Make sure it is truly perpendicular or the crank pin will bind and the bearing surface will quickly wear oversize.

FIGURE 49- PISTON ASSEMBLY

56

Assemble connecting rods, gudgeons and pistons as shown in figure 49. Make sure that pistons and cylinders are matched up and that the fit is very close but free of friction. Now is the time to perfect the fit.

Assemble the pistons, cylinders and connecting rods as in figure 50. It is possible that the connecting rods might rub on the cylinders so some adjustment may be required before the crank can make a full turn. The pistons must not touch the heads and the cylinders must not protrude beyond the inner edge of their supports.

FIGURE 50- POWER CYLINDER ASSEMBLY

TOE CLAMPS

These simple devices will hold work securely in place on the angle plate. Commercially they are made in many sizes and shapes but the small ones we need here are easy to make from mild steel bar stock. I used 3/16" X 5/8" bar that is used for stretching chainlink fence to make mine. Refer to figure 51 for details and dimensions. One screw is used to adjust the clamp parallel to the work piece surface and the other is used to draw it snugly against the workpiece. Hex head cap screws are indicated but socket head screws will be more convenient if you have them on hand. Note that one hole is tapped and the other is clearance size for the screw.

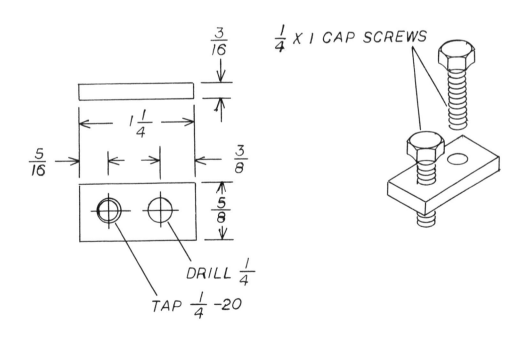

FIGURE 51- TOE CLAMPS

DETAIL 15 & 16 THE TRANSFER CYLINDER MOUNTS

Now comes two of the most demanding parts in the project. But they are not difficult to machine if you follow the correct sequence. The operations are all very basic and all of the lathe work is done with only two setups. You will need the angle plate and a couple of TOE CLAMPS to mount the castings.

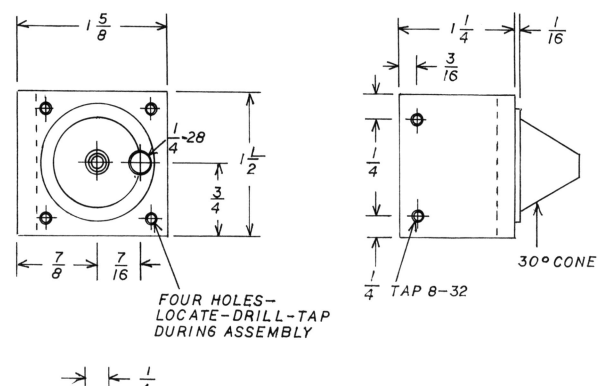

FOUR HOLES—
LOCATE-DRILL-TAP
DURING ASSEMBLY

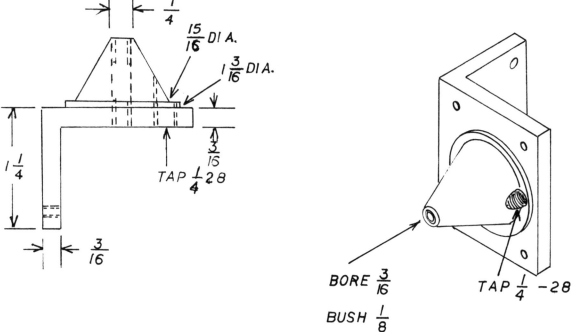

FIGURE 52- THE RIGHT TRANSFER CYLINDER MOUNT

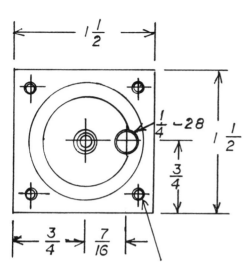

FOUR HOLES -
LOCATE - DRILL - TAP
DURING ASSEMBLY

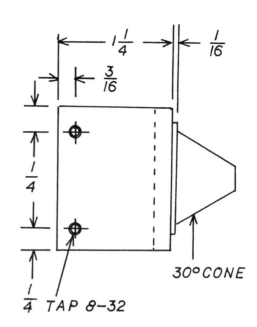

30° CONE

TAP 8-32

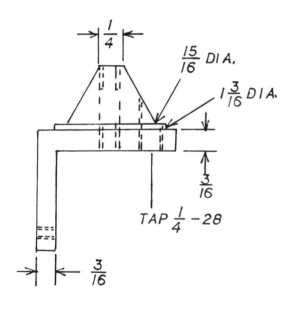

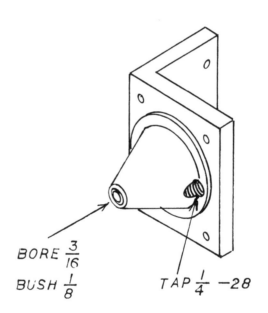

BORE $\frac{3}{16}$

BUSH $\frac{1}{8}$

TAP $\frac{1}{4}$ -28

FIGURE 53 THE LEFT TRANSFER CYLINDER MOUNT

The first operation after cleaning up the casting will be to face off the
surface of the mounting flange. Remember that the mounting flange portion
of the pattern was drafted but the leg of the angle that supports the cone
is of uniform thickness. So this flat surface is the first reference
surface we work from. We clamp the mount to the angle plate to face off
the outside surface of the mounting flange, which will then become the
reference surface for subsequent operations.

Figure 54 illustrates the setup for facing off the mounting flange. Two 1/4"-20 holes are tapped in the angle plate to accept the screws of the toe clamps. Clean up the casting with a coarse file before mounting. And make sure that there is a bit of clearance at the inside corner so that the piece rests properly on the angle plate. The thickness of the mounting flange is not critical. But face off only enough to clean up the mounting surface. The inside surface of the mounting flange does not mate with any other part so it does not require any machining.

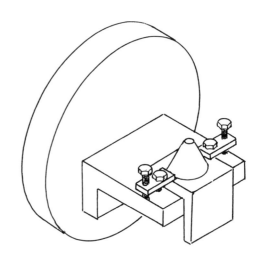

FIGURE 54

FIGURE 55

When the mounting flange has been faced off you can use the trysquare as a gauge to find the center of the cone as shown in figure 55. For the right mount the dimension is 7/8" and for the left it is 3/4" as indicated in the drawings. Layout die will help to make the mark more visible. Of course a surface plate and surface gauge would be more precise but such luxuries are usually not found in the home shop. Use a prick punch to mark the center clearly. Then clamp the mounting flange to the angle plate with the toe clamps as in figure 56.

The angle plate is loosened on the face plate and the tailstock can be brought up to center the work on the punch mark on the end of the cone. Rotate the faceplate by hand to ensure that the work is well centered before you tighten the angle plate securely. Make sure that the work protrudes far enough beyond the end of the angle plate so that all of the listed operations can be completed. Now think the entire series of operations through before you begin.

FIGURE 56

The following operations will include machining the cone with the compound slide set at 30 degrees, drilling and reaming the through hole and facing off the surface upon which the transfer cylinder flange mounts. There will also be a short shoulder that will locate the transfer cylinder bore. All of these diameters must be concentric so the second setup must be accurate and very secure. The order in which the operations is done is not important. But the setup can't be changed until all operations are complete. When you are certain that the setup is accurate and secure proceed to do the neccessary operations in any convenient order.

You might first turn the 1 3/16" diameter shoulder and face off the surface upon which the transfer cylinder flange will mount. Then machine the cone with the compound set at 30 degrees and face off the shoulder to its 1/16" height. Use the center drill to start the through hole and very carefully drill it 1/8" all the way through. Follow with an 11/64" bit and finish with a 3/16" reamer as shown in figure 57.

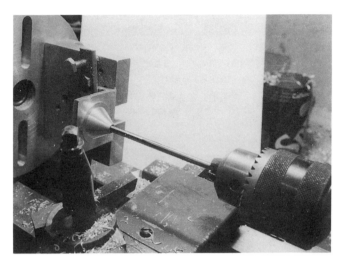

FIGURE 57

Now you can locate the center of the air transfer hole 7/16" from the center of the 3/16" through hole. Support the casting securely and drill the air transfer hole 7/32" and tap 1/4"-28. Of course it must be done from the inside surface of the angle. And it is always best to begin with a small hole, say 1/8", and enlarge in steps to the final size. The important thing in this step is that the hole remains inside the 1 3/16" diameter shoulder at the base of the cone.

THE TRANSFER PISTON ROD BUSHINGS

These bushings are not a standard hardware item so you will have to make them. Two are required in each transfer cylinder mount. They are 1/8" bore, a press fit in the 3/16" through hole and 1/4" long. Simply chuck a length of brass bar stock in the lathe and face off the end. Use the tailstock chuck to center and drill an undersize hole, say 7/64" or #33, about 3/4" deep. Follow with a 1/8" reamer. Turn the outside diameter to a light press fit in the through hole, which will be about .188" or .189". Lightly chamfer the end both inside and out and part off at 1/4". Again lightly chamfer the end both inside and out and part off the second bushing at 1/4". Press the bushings into each end of the mount and run the 1/8" reamer through. Try a length of 1/8" drill rod through the bore to ensure that it is a free fit. Work the drill rod in the bore to burnish the bushings until the fit is friction free when dry. This is a very important step because binding here could prevent the engine from running or at least impair efficiency. And if the fit is too loose the air leak would have the same effect.

61

The two 8-32 tapped holes in the mounting flange can be done now, but the remaining four tapped holes will be located with the aid of the transfer cylinder flange. At this time you can use the transfer cylinder mounts as a template to drill tap size holes in the base casting. Carefully locate and mark the horizontal center of the 7/8" hole in the base casting and clamp the mount in position with its center on the same line. The mounts will overlap the vertical edges of the base 3/8". Drill one hole through the tapped hole in the mount and through the base casting. Then enlarge the hole in the base casting and install one screw. Repeat for the second hole and you will be assured of proper alignment. Repeat for both mounts to assemble as in figure 58.

FIGURE 58

A pair of 1/8" drill rods through the mounts as shown in figure 59 will be an aid in aligning them for the second mounting screw hole. The object is to have the transfer piston rods running parallel and on the same center as the crank shaft. These mounting screws will not need to be accessible after assembly so they can be ordinary slotted or phillips heads.

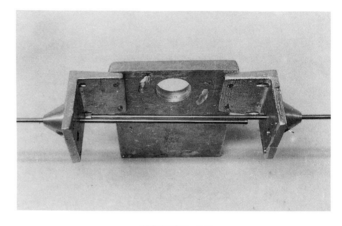

FIGURE 59

At this point you have a substantial number of the parts finished and you can make a trial assembly as shown in figure 60. You can also install the power assembly on the base casting. This will give you a reference as you finish parts and try them in their respective positions. The transfer piston rods will be custom finished by trial assembly so that the threads will not interfere with the motion of the rods.

FIGURE 60

DETAIL 17- THE TRANSFER PISTON ROD LINK

These are a delicate part but simple to make. Since they are very small
and the drilled holes must be accurately spaced the mating parts should be
stacked for all operations. It will be easiest if you lay out the hole
locations on stock somewhat longer than needed and then cut off the excess
after drilling. The spacers especially would be quite impossible to hold
for drilling. So you simply drill 7/64" holes through 1/16" X 1/4" stock
and then cut off the tiny squares with the hole centered.

The plates differ in that the back plate is drilled as indicated on the
drawing and the center hole is tapped 4-40. But the front plate has the
center hole enlarged to 7/64" to clear the 4-40 screw. The pins are 1/16"
drill rod and they are soft soldered in the back plates.

It will be easiest to do all of the drilling and tapping and solder in the
pins so that you can assemble the link before you form the radius on the
ends. Then you can use the enlarged tool rest on the grinder to form the
radius easily and uniformly. Dimensional details are in figure 61.

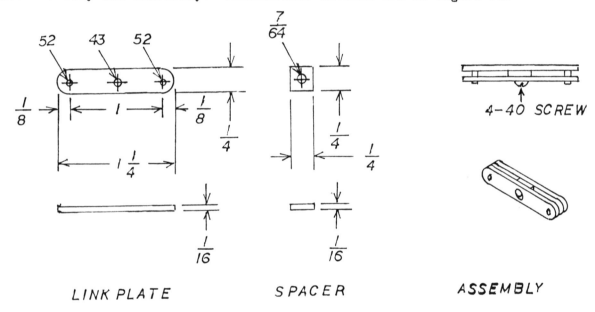

FIGURE 61- THE TRANSFER PISTON ROD LINK

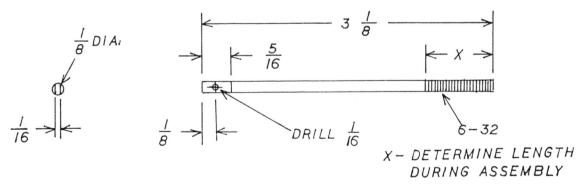

FIGURE 62- THE TRANSFER PISTON ROD

DETAIL 18- THE TRANSFER PISTON ROD

FIGURE 63

It would be difficult it not impossible to work 1/8" drill rod without some sort of holding fixture. The simple jig shown in figure 63 is a scrap of key stock with a 1/8" hole drilled through and a hacksaw slot to make it a clamp. A machine screw tightens the clamp to hold the work. This will enable you to clamp the work securely in the vise without damaging it while you file the flats and drill the 1/16" hole in the flatted end. It will also be a handy addition to your tool kit for future jobs.

Cut the rod to length as detailed in figure 62 and clamp it in the fixture as in figure 63. With 5/16" of the rod exposed beyond the clamp, use a safe edge file to reduce the thickness to .094". Rotate the work in the clamp 180 degrees and file the opposite side parallel to reduce the thickness to .062", which is close enough to 1/16". Very carefully mark and punch the pivot hole location. Rotate the work 90 degrees in the fixture and mount the fixture in the drilling vise to drill the 1/16" hole.

The rod and the link can now be installed in the engine to determine the length of the thread. With the transfer piston rod installed as seen in figure 64 you can measure the exposed amount for threading. The object is to make sure that no part of the thread will enter the bushing in the transfer cylinder mount. Mark the rod with file or scriber and remove it to cut 6-32 threads. Finish and install both rods now.

FIGURE 64

DETAIL 19- THE TRANSFER PISTON BASE

Like the transfer cylinder mounts, these require a bit of study. But don't feel intimidated because the setup is easy and the operations are routine. The casting has been designed with extra length on the shank so that it can easily be mounted in the chuck for machining. All of the operations must be done with one chucking so that all diameters will be concentric.

If the shank is not as smooth and clean as you would like you can first mount the casting by the base of the cone and true it up lightly. But the finish of the exterior of the shank is not important otherwise.

So with the casting mounted in the chuck as seen in figure 65 you can begin to machine it to dimensions in figure 66. The sequence is not important except to keep the tool changing to a minimum for efficiency. The inside of the cone is done with a boring bar. And you will want to use the transfer cylinder mounts as gauges to ensure that there is clearance when the base rests against the mount. Use the center drill to start the #33 through hole and tap 6-32 before parting off.

FIGURE 65

This is a rather delicate part so take plenty of time with each step and plan all of your moves carefully. Remember that developing skill is part of what this project is all about. The vital dimension is the diameter of the straight grooved shoulder that will push into the piston sleeve. And of course everything must be concentric and parallel because clearance in the transfer cylinder is slight.

DETAIL 20- THE TRANSFER PISTON

This is an easy boring and turning job, beginning with a length of standard 1" pipe. Done very much like the power cylinder. But we will braze a 1/32" plate on one end. Refer to figure 66 for dimensions. Note that the inside diameter is the same as the outside diameter of the shoulder on the transfer piston base.

Standard 1" pipe is sturdy enough so that it can be held in the chuck for turning and boring. But avoid over tightening the chuck, which would distort the work. If you use the four jaw chuck it will be best to center on the inside diameter rather than the outside diameter.

Use the heaviest boring bar you have for the job with a minimum of overhang. As with the power cylinder, the seam will make for rough cutting on the first couple of passes but it will soon clean up.

It is possible that thin tubing might be found near this size and in that case some labor could be saved. However at this writing a general source was not found so we held to the 1" pipe stock for the manual. But there is no reason why you could not modify the base to accomodate tubing if you have it available. And of course you might also find tubing that would serve for the cylinder as well. Keep in mind that increasing clearance between piston and cylinder will reduce power and efficiency.

First skim the inside diameter to no larger than 1.080" It does not matter if it is perfectly clean, but the seam should be removed. It will not matter if there is a slight air leak at the base.

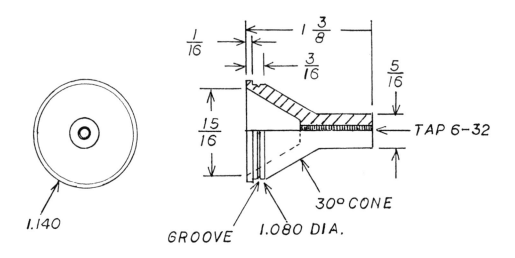

THE TRANSFER PISTON BASE DETAIL

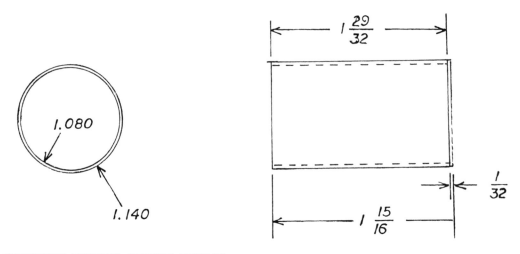

THE TRANSFER PISTON SLEEVE DETAIL

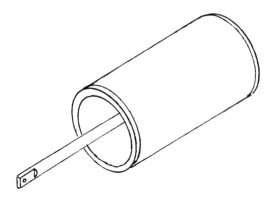

FIGURE 66- THE TRANSFER PISTON COMPONENTS

66

Then turn the outside diameter to 1.140", which will leave a wall thickness of .030" or about 1/32". Face off the end and chamfer slightly inside. Test the fit of the base but don't install it yet. Part off carefully at 1 29/32". The overall length of the assembled piston will include the length of the sleeve, the thickness of the end cover and the 1/16" shoulder of the base.

BRAZING THE PISTON ENDS

Cut a 1 1/2" square of 1/32" thick mild steel, making certain it remains flat and undistorted. Lay it on a fire brick or a very dry common brick and rest the parted end of the piston sleeve in its center. Carefully run a bead of brass all around the joint.

This work requires a neutral flame of the correct size to avoid burning through the 1/32" thick metal. An oxyacetylene torch is the preferred tool for this job but it can be done with some of the newer bottled gas torches. To achieve fusion with brass you need a bright red heat so that the spelter will flow through the joint for thorough bonding.

When the joint cools cut away as much of the excess as possible with snips. Be careful to avoid breaking or distorting the joint. Press the machined base into the open end and make about four punch marks at the rim to lock into the groove in the base. Then clamp the piston in the vise to file away the excess metal. Avoid beveling or rounding the end, which would thin the joint and weaken it.

FIGURE 67

When the joint is nearly finished you can chuck the piston in the lathe for the final polishing with file and abrasive. But be careful to avoid thinning the joint. Remember that you have only 1/32" thickness to work with. The finished pistons will appear as in figure 68. To the casual observer it will seem that such an item could not be made in the home shop with ordinary equipment.

FIGURE 68

The pistons can be screwed onto their rods temporarily but do not apply the thread locking compound until the final adjustment and assembly. The transfer cylinder mounts must be removed to drill and tap the holes for the flange screws.

DETAIL 21- THE TRANSFER CYLINDER

A short length of cylinder sleeve will be required as a gauge to drill the transfer cylinder mounts, so begin by chucking about 4 1/2" of standard 1" pipe in the lathe. Bore 1 3/16" and turn the outside diameter to 1 1/4". Face off and lightly chamfer the end and part off at 3 1/8". Again face off and part off the remainder to be used as a guage.

The flanges are made of 1 1/2" squares of 1/8" thick mild steel. Center carefully in the four jaw chuck and bore 1 1/4" for a snug friction fit over the cylinder sleeves. The flanges will be used as a drilling template so the four holes are drilled #29 at this time. They will later be enlarged to 11/64 to clear 8-32 screws.

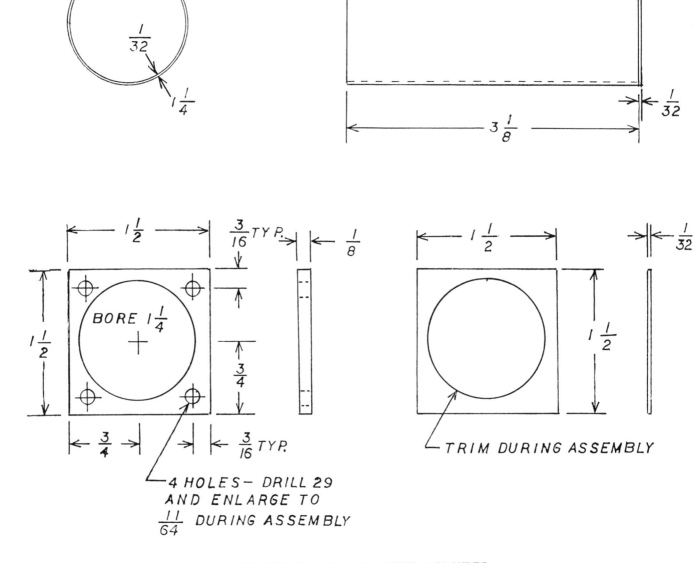

FIGURE 69- THE TRANSFER CYLINDER

68

Before the transfer cylinders are assembled use the prepared flanges to drill the tap size holes in the mounts as shown in figure 70. Clamp the mount in the drilling vise and slip the short sleeve into the flange so that it will be centered on the shoulder of the mount. Make certain that the flange does not shift as you drill the holes. And mark the flange so that it is brazed to the sleeve in proper orientation.

FIGURE 70

The remainder of the work on the cylinders will require some tests as we progress. So assemble the engine as shown in figure 71 and screw the flanges to the transfer cylinder mounts loosely. Now push the cylinder sleeves into the flanges and snug up the screws. operate the crank by hand to assure that the transfer pistons will move the entire stroke without rubbing the cylinder walls.

FIGURE 71

If the alignment is OK the sleeves can be brazed to the flanges as shown in figure 72. Make certain that the sleeve rests on the same plane as the flange so that alignment will be true. Remember that the flange is 1/8" thick while the cylinder is only 1/32" thick. So the flame is played more on the heavier metal to avoid burning through the cylinder. The object here is to sweat the joint so that the spelter will flow through. But avoid an excess of spelter, which will only add to the clean up. Also avoid running spelter into the holes. A liquid or paste silver solder flux can be used in the joint. And the holes could be filled with putty so that spelter would not bond.

FIGURE 72

The end of the cylinder is done just as with the piston. Cut flat 1 1/2" squares of 1/32" mild steel and braze them in place. Trim with the snips and finish with a file and abrasive cloth. Remember that the joints at base and end must be air tight. Cut thin gaskets to fit the flange, which will be used at final assembly.

The transfer pistons can now be installed permanently. Apply thread locking compound to the rod and screw the piston on so that when it is at the extreme inside stroke its base will clear the surface of the mount by 1/16" as seen in figure 73. Operate the crank by hand through several revolutions to confirm the adjustment. Once set do not disturb the setting or the bond of the thread lock compound will be spoiled. Read the directions if you are not familiar with using it.

FIGURE 73

Rotate the crank to travel the piston to the extreme outside stroke to make sure that it travels within the limit of the length of the transfer cylinder. Always check for binding and rubbing at each stage of assembly so that you will know what to do if problems arise in getting the engine running. If everything is Ok at this point you can remove the transfer piston rods and fill the rod bore with Vaseline petroleum jelly for final assembly. The transfer cylinders can be installed with gaskets but no shellac, which might enter the cylinder and cause problems.

FIGURE 74

DETAIL 22 & 23- THE AIR LINE ADAPTER AND AIR LINE

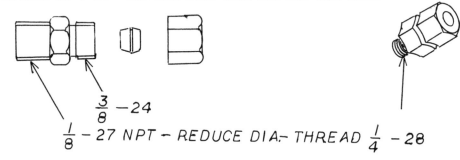

$\frac{3}{8}$ -24

$\frac{1}{8}$ - 27 NPT - REDUCE DIA.- THREAD $\frac{1}{4}$ - 28

FIGURE 75- THE AIR LINE ADAPTER

FIGURE 76

The base of a standard 3/16" compression sleeve adapter fitting is 1/8"-27 pipe thread. The sleeve end is 3/8"-24, which is standard S.A.E. thread. Chuck a scrap of sprue in the lathe and drill and tap 3/8" -24. Screw the brass fitting into the fixture and reduce the base to 1/4" and thread 1/4"-28. You can cut threads up to the shoulder by reversing the die after the first pass to start the threads. These will be straight threads so they will have to be sealed with thread lock compound or shellac on final assembly.

The air line is an 8" length of standard 3/16" copper tube. Be certain to ream the inside after cutting so that there is no restriction to the air.

DETAIL 24- THE ALCOHOL LAMP

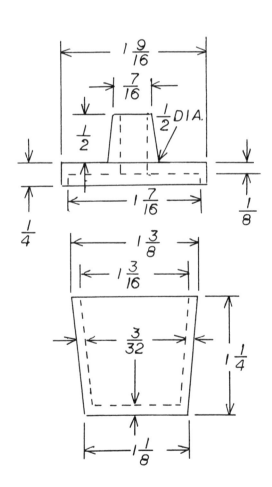

FIGURE 77- THE ALCOHOL LAMP

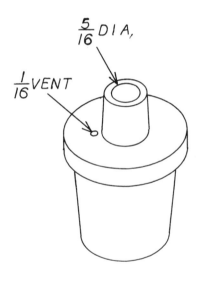

Very little work is required to finish the lamps. Simply chuck the lid and bore the 5/16" through hole. The 1/16" vent hole in the lid is important. Make a wick of cotton string to fill the bore snugly but not so tight as to restrict flow. It may be neccessary to clean up the rim of the pot and the inside of the lid. But the fit between pot and lid does not have to be perfect.

At this point you have completed the engine as seen in figure 78. The air lines can be installed now. Bend them carefully to avoid kinking. And avoid changing the bend many times, which will work harden the copper and increase the tendency to kink. Copper can be annealed by heating to red heat and quenching in water. But if you anneal it be sure to blow out any scale that forms on the inside and dry out the water. If there is any rubbing or binding correct the problem now. It will be a good idea to belt the engine to a small motor and run it in for a period of time. Lubricate before you begin with very light oil, such as sewing machine oil.

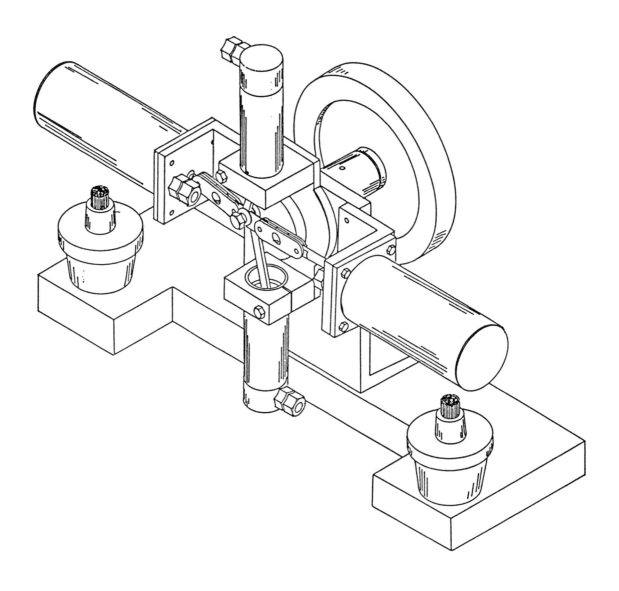

FIGURE 78

DETAIL 25- THE COOLING FINS

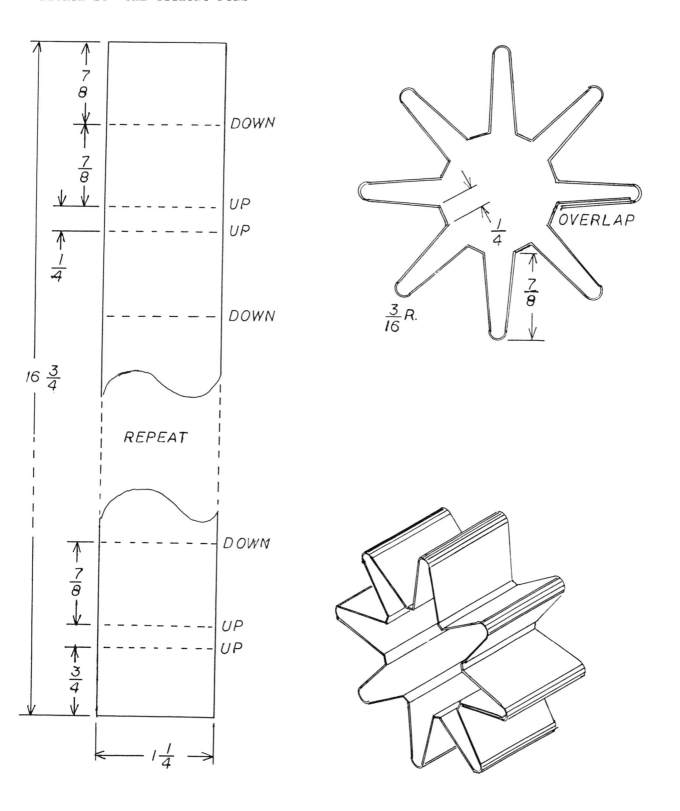

FIGURE 79- THE COOLING FINS

The cooling fins are a simple sheet metal job. Use thin gauge aluminum or galvanized metal. Roof flashing material is ideal. Simply cut a strip 1 1/4" wide and 16 3/4" long. Mark the bend points with a prick punch so that you can see them from both sides. Bend alternately up and down in the repeated pattern indicated in figure 79. The overlap does not have to be fastened in any way. If a brake is not available use a needle nose pliers or improvise a tool by cutting a slot in a scrap of key stock to make sharp bends where contact is made with the cylinder. The outside points can be sharp or round. Adjust the tension by hand and slip the fins over the cylinder.

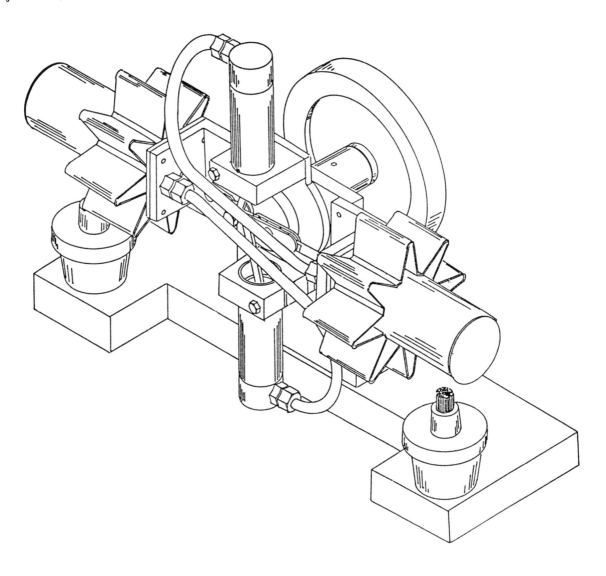

FIGURE 80- THE ENGINE COMPLETE

Alcohol lamps are a simple device and there is no danger of explosion when used properly. But there is a definite fire hazard because alcohol is very flammable and volatile. It burns with a non-luminous flame that is almost invisible in daylight. If it runs through a crack or hole in the floor it can start a fire that will destroy an entire structure quickly.

The first rule of safety is to close the container you use to fill the lamps and move it a safe distance away before you light the lamps. And make certain to wipe up any spills and dispose of the rag safely before you light the lamps. A trail of drips from the lamp to an open storage container can result in an explosion and a serious fire. And make certain that the engine and the lamps are in no danger of being knocked over.

The lamps in this project are very rudimentary and it is obvious that if tipped over when ignited the burning fuel will ignite anything it comes in contact with. Even an ounce of burning alcohol can start a serious fire and cause injuries that could be fatal.

Because they are made of aluminum these lamps will conduct heat and if used for long periods they will over heat and vaporize the fuel, which will then begin to burn around the lid. Simply blow out the flame and let them cool down. They will be too hot to handle so don't try to pick them up. It is also an indication that the pot is nearly empty if it begins to burn around the lid so it is time to blow them out anyway. Another indication that they are nearly out of fuel is when the wick begins to glow red.

The best practice is to fill the pots no more than two thirds with alcohol and let them get cool enough to touch before refilling.

Except for the transfer piston rods, which are lubricated with Vaseline petroleum jelly, all moving parts should be given a drop of very light oil. Sewing machine oil, household oil or utility oil is OK. Heavy oils will be too stiff and interfere with operation. Do not lubricate too often or too heavily or the oil may be drawn into the cylinders. Occasionaly dab a bit of Vaseline on the transfer piston rods while the engine is running and it will be drawn in. The lower power cylinder is easy to oil while the engine is running but the engine will have to be inverted to oil the upper cylinder. You can drill a 1/16" hole in the upper cylinder just above the mount if you want to add an occasional drop of oil while running. Slant the hole downward and be sure to deburr the inside so the piston is not damaged.

When everything is properly fit and aligned the flywheel will spin freely by hand and coast for a revolution or so. Normal rotation is counter clockwise when viewed from the cylinder side. If everything is properly aligned but a little stiff you can run it in by belting to a small motor such as a sewing machine motor or a small fan motor.

I built some of my earlier hot air engines with fits a bit too snug and so had to use a propane torch for extra heat until they ran in. There is some danger of melting the braze joint on the cylinder end if you use the propane torch.

Possible areas of trouble will be air leaks or excess friction in bearings or pivots. If the leak is at the cylinder end simply re-braze it and dress down with a file. You can adapt a small hose to the air line to apply a bit of pressure to test for a leak with soap solution.

Begin with the power cylinders at 90 degrees as shown in the drawings. It will take from one to three minutes for the engine to run after you light the fires. Both fires must be lit. It will not start until the transfer piston displaces some air to raise or lower the pressure, so you will have to give it a slight turn to start. Once started it will gradually increase in speed. When it is running freely you can loosen the clamp screws and rotate the power cylinder assembly slowly clockwise until the speed no longer increases. That is the optimum setting of the phase relationship between transfer and power cylinders so tighten the clamp screws and sit back and enjoy your engine.

Congratulations! You have built a running engine. Now you can set up to produce several at once on a mini-assembly line. Or you can begin research and experimentation to develop a truly practical and useful Stirling Cycle engine. Do not suppose that nothing is left to be discovered or that you would not be the one to do it. Document your work with notes and sketches as you go for your own reference and for others who might follow. It is in just that way that the engines of the future will be developed.